Vows & Toasts

SELLERS
PUBLISHING

President & Publisher: Ronnie Sellers
Publishing Director: Robin Haywood
Managing Editor: Mary Baldwin
Senior Editor: Megan Hiller
Assistant Production Editor: Charlotte Smith

Published by Sellers Publishing, Inc.
161 John Roberts Road • South Portland, ME 04106
(800) 625-3386 toll free
Visit our Web site: www.rsvp.com • E-mail: rsp@rsvp.com

Wiccan Handfasting Ceremony (p. 79) © 1994, Mary A. Axford.
Please note: Every attempt has been made to contact current copyright holders. Any omission is unintentional and the publisher
welcomes hearing from any copyright holders not acknowledged in this book. Omissions will be corrected in subsequent printings.

Library of Congress control number: 2007926827
ISBN 13: 978-1-56906-990-5

Manufactured in India.

10 9 8 7 6 5 4 3 2 1

Vows & Toasts

Hundreds of Ways to Say I Do and Here's to You!

from the editors at Sellers Publishing, Inc.

photographs by Carol Ross

CONTENTS

INTRODUCTION

As the editors who brought you *The Bride's Year Ahead*, *The Mother of the Bride*, and *The Groom's Guide*, we understand the importance and meaning of the vows you will say on your wedding day. With that pinnacle moment in mind, we offer you this book, *Vows & Toasts*, to assist you in making your vows exactly what you want them to be and to help your loved ones to toast you in their own special way.

Part One of this book offers a comprehensive section on wedding vows that explores numerous different traditional and nontraditional vow options. The vast selection of sample vows represents various denominations from many different faiths and cultures. Readers also will find a handful of ceremonies and rituals that can be included in any wedding ceremony, regardless of a couple's faith or background. We've also included information on second-time marriage vows, renewal vows, and detailed material for those brides and grooms wishing to write their own wedding vows.

Part Two assists readers looking for guidance in making the perfect wedding toast. Whether you're the father of the bride, the best man, the bride or groom, or a family member or friend with sentiments you wish to express to the happy couple, this book will advise you of proper toasting etiquette, how to prepare and deliver the toast, and when and where a toast is appropriate, as well as give you the tools and information you need to pull the right words and thoughts together for the special day.

PART ONE

WEDDING VOWS

The words that a couple chooses to use in their wedding vows are meant to lay the groundwork for their lives together and to strengthen their marriage for a lifetime. The most basic definition of a marriage vow is a promise two people make to one another, expressing unconditional love — "in sickness and in health" and "for richer or for poorer." In most Western wedding ceremonies, it is common for the couple to repeat vows of love and support, even going so far as to say "till death do us part." However, this is not a tradition that is practiced around the world, as many cultures have entirely different or, at the very least, additional ways of expressing love and commitment.

The vows that couples exchange are just one part of the wedding ceremony. A traditional ceremony includes: the wedding processional (the entrance of the entire wedding party, traditionally up the aisle); readings from the Bible, a prayer, literature, poetry, or a specially written piece for the event; the wedding vows; the exchange of rings; the blessing (either the official sanction by the officiant or from a member or two of the wedding party); the first kiss of the newly joined couple; and finally, the recessional. Part one of this book includes a number of traditional and nontraditional vows, as well as some rituals and ceremonies you may consider incorporating into your larger wedding ceremony. The section wraps up with information on writing your own vows.

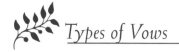 *Types of Vows*

The language of marriage vows has varied over the years as much as the two people exchanging them. Every religion, culture, and country has different wedding vows and traditions. And every couple wants a ceremony that is uniquely theirs. However, vows do fall into some basic categories.

Many vows fall under the banner of tradition, in which the ending is usually the famous "I do." Traditional vows follow the time-honored language of a couple's faith or heritage. Nontraditional ceremonies include many types of customized vows and rituals chosen by the bride and groom, either together or separately, after discussing the main focus and mood of the celebration. Nontraditional vows might be appropriate for interfaith, intercultural, or second-time marriages. They might incorporate some rituals and language from other traditions, or they might be written entirely by the couple.

Today, more couples are deciding to write their own vows in order to personalize the wedding not only for themselves, but for their families and guests as well. When writing personal vows, there are many ways in which to make the day special — from incorporating a certain ethnic flavor to choosing a favorite poem, song, quote, or prayer, almost anything goes in the modern ceremony.

Although many couples are becoming more comfortable in expressing their undying love to the world, others are more reserved or may simply prefer the time-honored language of traditional vows. So, while all brides and grooms will be excited about planning their wedding vows for that special day, many will opt for an established, familiar type of ceremony. The key things any couple should keep in mind are the tone they would like to set, the mood they want to convey, and, most important, the style that fits them best. Whether the vows are traditional, nontraditional, or something special they have written themselves, these are words that are meant to last a lifetime.

Choosing the Right Vows for You

Deciding on the perfect vows can be a daunting task. Whether traditional or contemporary, created from the heart or passed down through one's religious affiliation, wedding vows are the beginning of a couple's life together. As the years pass and a marriage becomes more cemented in love and trust, the one thing that a couple can always share is the memory of those special words that were spoken on that first day as husband and wife.

It's true that planning a wedding is hard work, and anything you can do to make it easier seems like a good idea. But don't skimp on the time to discuss this most important part of the ceremony and choose the right vows for you, regardless of whether you write them yourselves or look for just the right traditional words of love. You might start by looking at existing vows from various religions and cultures, and then altering the words as you wish. If you and your spouse are of different religions, you might want to come up with a way to incorporate both religious traditions into your big day. Even though finding the right wedding vows for you certainly takes time, your ceremony will be more meaningful as a result. If you decide to write your own vows, the time you spend crafting them will forge a special bond between you as

a couple, and your words will also say much to the guests about your union.

Vow Traditions

There are many different kinds of vows and many different types of wedding ceremonies, reflecting religions and cultures around the globe. From the Christian faith to the Jewish, Hindu, and Buddhist religions, to everything in between, wedding vows encompass a world of traditions.

Christians see marriage as a sacred union and believe that two people must stay together through the trials and tribulations that come with life. If you prefer a traditional Christian wedding, you can have the minister or wedding official find the right words, or you can write your own and incorporate them into the ceremony. The most commonly used wedding vows from the Christian religion are from the Anglican Church's 1662 *Book of Common Prayer*. Almost everyone is familiar with these words:

I, [bride's name], take thee, [groom's name], to be my wedded husband, to have and to hold from this day forward, for better or for worse, for richer or for poorer, in sickness and in health, to love and to cherish, till death do us part.

In the Jewish religion, marriage is a very important and sacred union because it enables the race to continue indefinitely. With this in mind, marriage is considered a directive of sorts. While you will never hear the words "I do" in a Jewish wedding, a Jewish ceremony nevertheless has a distinctive tradition and style. But as with other religions, there are many variations within that tradition. Couples are allowed to exchange personal wedding vows if they choose. The various Jewish denominations, from Orthodox to Conservative to Reformed, may all have a slightly different way of celebrating the wedding day. Many Orthodox and Conservative Jewish wedding ceremonies are conducted in Hebrew.

When exchanging your vows, you'll want to make sure your guests know what is being said, so consider handouts with translations — especially for the part that involves the vows. Jewish weddings traditionally have two parts: kiddushin, the betrothal ceremony, and nissuin, which is the wedding ceremony. During the betrothal ceremony, the groom usually gives his bride a ring.

The actual wedding ceremony is concentrated on the seven blessings for the couple. This celebrates the marriage of the two people and thanks God for the union.

Muslim marriages are often still arranged by the parents, and the vows reflect this as well. Islam teaches that marriage is the foundation of society. Muslim weddings can last from four to seven days, and many rituals are celebrated. Normally during the traditional Muslim ceremony the official discusses with the bride and groom what marriage means, and then the bride and groom give their consent for marriage. However, this is not the formal exchange of vows. After both bride and groom give their consent, the traditional exchange begins. The typical wording includes these statements from the bride:

I, [name], offer you myself in marriage in accordance with the instructions of the Holy Koran and the Holy Prophet, peace and blessing be upon him. I pledge, in honesty and with sincerity, to be for you an obedient and faithful wife.

The groom then says:

I pledge, in honesty and with sincerity, to be for you a faithful and helpful husband.

The Koran addresses the importance of marriage for all Muslims; it says, "And among His signs is this, that He created for you mates from among yourselves, that you may dwell in tranquility with them, and He has put love and mercy between your hearts."

Several Eastern religions celebrate particular styles of wedding ceremonies and vows, the most notable being Hinduism and Buddhism. Hindu weddings are often festive and colorful affairs, and the actual wedding can last up to three hours. Buddhist wedding ceremonies are considered more secular since there is no particular religious implication. In fact, there is no traditional Buddhist ceremony for a wedding; rather, rituals such as the lighting of incense and offerings to Buddha are always a part of the exchange of vows. In a Buddhist wedding ceremony, vows from the Buddhist guide for the domestic and social life of a layman, the "Sigalovada Sutta," are usually used.

Secular weddings are usually the type of ceremony that a bride and groom will choose if neither is particularly religious. Secular wedding vows center more on the couple's faith in one another than on religious belief; however, it is not uncommon for some religious vows to be a part of the ceremony. Secular wedding vows might include wording like this:

I, [name], take you, [name], to be my husband/ wife. I promise to be true to you and only you, to love and trust and honor you. I will share your sorrows and shoulder your sorrows, be a calming presence in your life for both the good times and the bad.

Sometimes secular vows highlight the couple's view of marriage — the bride and groom may talk about marrying their best friend, and the wedding ceremony allows them to make a promise to one another in the presence of loved ones.

Whatever the vows, secular ceremonies tend to be quite simple. While the ceremony certainly can include traditional rituals, just as in religious ceremonies, the bride and groom have the freedom to do as they please and exchange whatever vows they see fit for their big day.

In addition to the more common religions around the world, many smaller religious sects or cultural groups also have their own religious ceremonies; these are often quite elaborate and may

include unique vows. Sometimes honoring your family's heritage is a good reason to seek out such special vows; they can add a distinctive feature to the ceremony that is especially meaningful to you and your family. The Greek Orthodox ceremony, for instance, has an unusual exchange of vows: the couple does not say anything as they exchange rings, walk around the altar, and drink from the same cup, all in silence. In a Shinto Japanese ceremony, the couple exchanges the vows while both sets of parents face one another in a show of the two families becoming one. The bride and groom also do what is called San-san-kudo, the exchanging of the nuptial cups. "Jumping the broom" is a well-known part of the vow ceremony in African weddings. The Celtic heritage also has a rich tradition of special vows, such as this simple but memorable promise:

I vow to you the first cut of my meat, the first sip of my wine; from this day on it shall be only your name I cry out in the night and into your eyes that I smile each morning…

VOW INNOVATIONS

One of the major trends in marriage ceremonies is for couples to write their own vows. Writing your own wedding vows can be a nerve-wracking experience even for the most confident of individuals. Will you write them down and read them? Will you memorize them? Will you say your written vows in conjunction with more traditional vows, or will the vows you and your spouse create be the only ones used during the entire ceremony?

Also, before you sit down to work on your vows, decide whether you want to write them separately or together. Sometimes couples even choose

to surprise one another. Think about your past, your future, and what you have done as a couple; where you have been and where you are going. What special moments have you shared together? Maybe that first kiss was the initial sign of the depth of your feelings for one another.

Think about what marriage means to you, what you expect from your future partner, and what, in turn your spouse can expect from you. All of these things may figure deeply in the words you choose to say to one another in front of your family and friends.

Remember, too, to determine if the vows you want to recite at your ceremony will be acceptable in the place you are getting married. Some churches and clergy have very strict rules about what can and can't be done. Changing the wording in religious vows may not be permitted. This is due, in part, to the fact that religion often plays a huge role in the marriage ceremony, and it is a main focus for many couples. Some officiants do not want to deviate from the church's traditional vows, so be sure to learn your clergy's thoughts on the matter before you begin to write your own vows.

Also think carefully about who will perform your ceremony. If he or she does not have the same general ideas and beliefs as you and your spouse, then you should continue to look for the right person. It is very important that the wedding vows exchanged between you and your spouse match your personality, your feelings, and your beliefs in one another and your new life together. You would not compromise on the church, the reception, or anything else regarding your ceremony, so do not settle on an officiant and his or

her particular vows either, unless they truly match your own.

Other wedding innovations don't involve completely original vows, but some kind of personal expression, or even participation by the guests. Often couples incorporate their personalities into the wedding vows; this can include adding a favorite poem or song. You might even want to involve the guests in the ceremony. For example, after the vows, have all the guests release butterflies or blow bubbles to send good blessings out into the world.

Keep in mind when writing your vows that while your wedding should be solemn on some levels, it is also important to have a good time. This is the first day of your life together as husband and wife, and regardless of your religious views, there is something sacred about that journey. But also feel free to express yourself through your vows and savor the moment, since this will be one of the happiest days of your life.

Deciding to renew your wedding vows can also be a beautiful thing. When two people who

have been married for quite a long time say "I do" again, it means not only that they still love one another, but that they still believe in everything they did years ago. Perhaps you didn't write your own vows the first time and regretted it later. It doesn't really matter when you decide to renew your vows, be it after the first year, the tenth, or the fiftieth. There certainly is never a wrong time to say all over again that you love your life partner. It also does not matter if you do so in front of family and friends or just for each other. Some people take their old wedding vows and add to them, including thoughts about all the changes they have encountered since they first got married and how they have endured to come out even stronger. If you have children, you might want to include them in your renewal ceremony. This is certainly a special moment for them as well as the two of you, knowing that their parents still love each other today as much as they did so many years ago.

# Traditional Vows

The choice of vows is one of the most important decisions you will make regarding your wedding. Therefore, when planning what your vow exchange will be, you want to know exactly what you are saying and why. If you are getting married in a church or synagogue, the clergy can of course advise you on the vow options customary in your faith. One of the most common traditional Christian marriage vows is the "Form of Solemnization of Matrimony" from the Anglican *Book of Common Prayer*. Everyone has heard this opening phrase:

> *Dearly beloved, we are gathered together here in the sight of God, and in the face of this congregation, to join together this man and this woman in holy matrimony.*

Often a bride and groom choose to have a religious wedding, but for various reasons do not want the standard vows from a particular denomination.

There are many traditional wedding vows for nondenominational marriage ceremonies. The ones most often used are the Declaration of Intent and the standard civil ceremony (see p. 66), which will be discussed in a later section. The Declaration of Intent was originally from medieval Christian ceremonies, and literally means the officiant asks the intention of the bride and the groom:

> *Will you have this woman/man to be your wedded wife/husband, to live together in the holy estate of matrimony? Will you love her, comfort her, honor, and keep her, in sickness and in health?*

Other forms of traditional wedding vows and customs are also used. The Blessing and Exchange of Rings ceremony celebrates the symbol of the rings as an external manifestation of an inner spiritual bond. This is the origin of the phrase "With this ring, I thee wed." The rings are a token of an unbroken circle of love that is both given and received.

The following pages offer examples of Christian vows, including Catholic, Protestant, Anglican, and Orthodox as well as Jewish ceremonies.

Traditional Christian Vows

Christianity, like all religions, is complex. Over time Christianity has become composed of, but not necessarily limited to, three major divisions: Catholic, Protestant (and some would add Anglican), and Orthodox. Within each of these divisions there are many denominations. Each one has its own distinctive beliefs or practices, but they are commonly considered branches of the same religion because they basically agree on such fundamentals as the Bible, the Trinity, and the teachings of the Nicene Creed.

One of the main ideas behind the Christian religious vows is that of joining man and woman together as one. Given the story of Adam and Eve, Christians believe that marriage is an institution that God wants men and women to experience. However, there are many different denominations as noted above, and therefore many ways that Christian couples exchange vows. The traditional Christian marriage ceremony often begins with the words "Dearly beloved, we are gathered here in the sight of God," but this is certainly not mandatory.

The "Form of Solemnization of Matrimony" from the Anglican *Book of Common Prayer* includes different vows for the bride and groom, with the man promising to "love and protect" and the woman promising to "serve and obey." Many modern ceremonies amend these vows to indicate equality between the sexes, usually with identical vows such as "love, honor, and protect" spoken by both.

The ceremony explains the three reasons that marriage was ordained in the tradition of the Apostle Paul (procreation, remedy against sin, and mutual society), and both the congregation and the couple are asked if there is any reason they should not be joined in marriage.

Following is an abbreviated version of a much longer text. Couples can add to or modify these vows as desired.

At the day and time appointed for solemnization of matrimony, the persons to be married shall come into the church with their friends and neighbors; and there standing together, the man on the right hand, and the woman on the left, with that person who shall give the woman betwixt them, the officiant shall say:

OFFICIANT: Dearly beloved, we are gathered together here in the sight of God to join together this man and this woman in holy matrimony; which is an honorable estate, instituted of God in Paradise, and into which holy estate these two persons present come now to be joined.

Therefore if any man can show any just cause, why they may not lawfully be joined together, let him now speak, or else hereafter for ever hold his peace.

I require and charge you both, as ye will answer at the dreadful day of judgment when the secrets of all hearts shall be disclosed, that if either of you know any impediment, why ye may not be lawfully joined together in matrimony, that ye confess it. For ye be well assured, that so many as be coupled together otherwise than God's word doth allow are not joined together by God; neither is their

matrimony lawful. At which day of marriage, if any man do allege and declare any impediment, why they may not be coupled together in matrimony, by God's law, or the laws of the realm; and will be bound, and sufficient sureties with him, to the parties; or else put in a caution (to the full value of such charges as the persons to be married do thereby sustain)

to prove his allegation; then the solemnization must be deferred, until such time as the truth be tried.

If no impediment be alleged, then shall the officiant say to the man:

OFFICIANT TO GROOM: Wilt thee have this woman to be thy wedded wife, to live together after God's ordinance in the holy estate of matrimony? Wilt thee love her, comfort her, honor, protect, and keep her, in sickness and in health; and, forsaking all other's, keep thee only unto her, so long as ye both shall live?

GROOM: I will.

OFFICIANT TO BRIDE: Wilt thee have this man to be thy wedded husband, to live together after God's ordinance in the holy estate of matrimony? Wilt thee protect him, and serve him, love, honor, and keep him in sickness and in health; and, forsaking all other's, keep thee only unto him, so long as ye both shall live?

BRIDE: I will.

Thus ends the formal betrothal. The couple shall advance to the altar, led by the officiant, who shall then turn to the assembled company, and say:

OFFICIANT: Who giveth this woman to be married to this man?

The person who gives the woman shall answer, and shall place the woman's right hand in the hand of the officiant, and then shall retire. Then shall they give their troth to each other in this manner: The officiant, receiving the woman at her father's or friend's hands, shall cause the groom with his right hand to take the bride by her right hand, and to say after him as followeth:

GROOM: I, _____, take thee, _____, to be my wedded wife, to have and to hold from this day forward, for better for worse, for richer for poorer, for fairer or fouler, in sickness and in health, to love and to cherish, till death us do part, according to God's holy ordinance; and thereunto I plight thee my troth.

Then shall they loose their hands; and the bride, with her right hand taking the groom by his right hand, shall likewise say after the officiant:

BRIDE: I, _____, take thee, _____, to be my wedded husband, to have and to hold from this day forward, for better for worse, for richer for poorer, in sickness and in health, to love and to cherish, till death us do part, according to God's holy ordinance; and thereunto I plight thee my troth.

Then shall they again loose their hands; and the groom shall give unto the bride a ring, laying the same upon the book with the accustomed duty to the officiant. And the officiant shall bless the ring(s) in the following manner:

OFFICIANT: Bless these rings, O merciful Lord, that those who wear them, that give and receive them, may be ever faithful to one another, remain in your peace, and live and grow old together in your love, under their own vine and fig tree, and seeing their children's children. Amen.

And the officiant, taking the ring, shall deliver it to the groom, to put it on the fourth finger of the bride's left hand. And the groom holding the ring there, and taught by the officiant, shall say:

GROOM: With this ring I thee wed, [*here placing it upon her thumb*] and with my body I thee honor, [*here placing it upon her index finger*] and with all my worldly goods I thee endow: [*here placing it upon her ring finger*] In the Name of the Father, and of the Son, and of the Holy Spirit. Amen.

If it be a double-ring ceremony, let the bride do the same as the groom, giving the groom the ring, and repeating the same words as he. They both shall kneel down; and the officiant shall say:

OFFICIANT: Let us pray. O Eternal God, creator and preserver of all mankind, Giver of all spiritual grace, the Author of everlasting life; Send thy blessing upon these thy servants, this man and this woman, whom we bless in thy Name; that, as Isaac and Rebecca lived faithfully together, so these persons may surely perform and keep the vow and covenant betwixt them

made, whereof this ring given and received is a token and pledge, and may ever hereafter remain in perfect love and peace together, and live according to thy laws; through Jesus Christ our Lord. Amen.

God the Father, God the Son, God the Holy Spirit, bless, preserve, and keep you; the Lord mercifully with his favor look upon you; and so fill you with all spiritual benediction and grace, that ye may so live together in this life, that in the world to come ye may have life everlasting. Amen.

And here shall be said the Lord's Prayer. Then shall the officiant join their right hands together, and say:

OFFICIANT: Those whom God hath joined together let no man put asunder.

Then shall the officiant speak unto the people.

OFFICIANT: Forasmuch as _____ and _____ have consented together in holy wedlock, and have witnessed the same before God and this company, and thereto have given and pledged their troth each to the other, and have declared the same by giving and receiving of a ring, and by joining of hands; I pronounce therefore that they be husband and wife together, in the Name of the Father, and of the Son, and of the Holy Spirit. Amen.

Traditional Catholic Vows

The Roman Catholic Church believes that the exchange of wedding vows is the most important part of the sacred tradition of marriage. The ceremony and its workings are more precise than in other religions; however, the couple still has certain options to choose from in terms of the officiant presenting the vows. In the most traditional form, the officiant asks questions of the bride and groom individually, to which they respond "I do." The officiant may also say the vows and the couple can repeat them, or the couple can recite the lines themselves, either from memory or reading from a prompt.

The vow exchange between the bride and groom happens in the middle of three traditional rites: the Nuptials, the Solemn Promise, and the Blessing and Exchange of Rings. There are many other details of the ceremony, but as with any tradition, the spoken promises between the betrothed couple are the heart, the soul, and the essence of the Catholic wedding ceremony. Even within a traditional framework, it is possible to choose the presentation of your Catholic wedding vows to best suit you.

During the rite of the Nuptials, the officiant individually asks the bride and groom if they have come of their own free will to unite with the other

For the Solemn Promise, the officiant asks the couple to join their right hands and declare their promise before God and the Church. They then take their wedding vows after which the priest blesses them, joins them together in marriage, and recites a second blessing: "May the Lord in His goodness strengthen your consent and fill you both with His blessings. What God has joined together, let no man put asunder."

The priest blesses the wedding rings as symbols of deep faith and peace, and the bride and groom exchange them with a pledge of unconditional love and fidelity.

■ EXAMPLES ■

❧No. 1

BRIDE/GROOM: I, _____, take you, _____, for my lawful husband/wife, to have and to hold, from this day forward, for better, for worse, for richer, for poorer, in sickness and health, until death do us part.

❧No. 2

BRIDE/GROOM: I, _____, take you, _____, to be my husband/wife. I promise to be true to you in good times and in bad, in sickness and in health. I will love and honor you all the days of my life.

in marriage. This questioning, before all who are in attendance, formally establishes that the couple is indeed free to marry and comes to the marriage with the right intent. The ritual suggests the question is asked, and the priest elicits a response from bride and groom in turn, not together.

The officiant then asks if they will honor and love one another as husband and wife for the rest of their lives, and if they will accept children from God lovingly and bring them up according to the law of Christ and his Church.

PRIEST: Do you take _____ as your lawful wife/husband, to have and to hold, from this day forward, for better or for worse, for richer or for poorer, in sickness and in health, to love and cherish until death do you part?

BRIDE/GROOM: I do.

I take this ring as a sign of my love and faithfulness in the name of the Father, the Son, and the Holy Spirit.

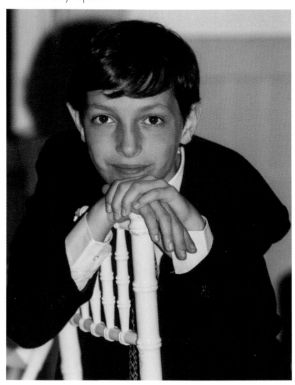

Traditional Protestant Vows

The Protestant wedding ceremony, like other Christian wedding ceremonies, is a worship service through which the will of God is served and Jesus as Lord is proclaimed. (There are some exceptions to this belief, such as in some Unitarian-Universalist and Quaker congregations.) The wedding guests are often participants in the service by sharing in hymns, scriptural readings, and responses to the couple's exchange of vows. Examples of vows from many specific Protestant denominations follow.

OFFICIANT: Dearly beloved friends, we are gathered here in the sight of God and in the face of this company, to join together this man and this woman in holy matrimony; which is an honorable estate, instituted of God in Paradise, in the time of man's innocency, signifying unto us the mystical union that is betwixt Christ and His Church and therefore is not by any to be enterprised nor taken in hand unadvisedly or lightly; but reverently, discreetly, advisedly, and soberly, duly considering the causes for which matrimony was ordained: One was the procreation of children.

It was also ordained for the mutual society, help, and comfort that the one ought to have for the other, both in prosperity and adversity; into which holy estate these two persons present come now to be joined. Therefore, if any person can show just cause why they may not lawfully be joined together, let them speak now, or else hereafter for ever hold their peace.

OFFICIANT (addressing the congregation): Will all of you witnessing these promises do all in your power to uphold these two persons in their marriage?

CONGREGATION: We will.

OFFICIANT: Who gives this woman to be married to this man?

FATHER OF THE BRIDE: She gives herself, with the blessing of her mother and father.

(A hymn, song, or reading may follow.)

TO THE BRIDE/GROOM: Wilt thou have this man/woman to be thy wedded husband/wife, to live together after God's ordinance in the holy estate of matrimony? Wilt thou love him/her, comfort him/her, honor and keep him/her, in sickness and in health? And forsaking all others, keep thee only unto him/her, so long as ye both shall live?

BRIDE/GROOM: I will.

The groom faces the bride and he takes her right hand in his.

GROOM: In the name of God, I, _____, take you, _____, to be my wife, to have and to hold from this day forward, for better, for worse, for richer, for poorer, in sickness and in health, to love and to cherish, until we are parted by death. This is my solemn vow.

They drop hands. The bride then takes his right hand in hers.

BRIDE: In the name of God, I, _____, take you, _____, to be my husband, to have and to hold form this day forward, for better, for worse, for richer, for poorer, in sickness and in health, to love and to cherish, until we are parted by death. This is my solemn vow.

They drop hands.

OFFICIANT: Bless, O Lord, these rings as a symbol of the vows by which this man and this woman have bound themselves to each other; through Jesus Christ our Lord.

CONGREGATION: Amen.

The groom places the ring on the ring finger of the bride's left hand.

GROOM: I give you this ring as a symbol of my love, and with all that I am, and all that I have, I honor you, in the Name of the Father, and of the Son, and of the Holy Spirit.

The bride places the ring on the ring finger of the groom's left hand.

BRIDE: I give you this ring as a symbol of my love, and with all that I am, and all that I have, I honor you, in the Name of the Father, and of the Son, and of the Holy Spirit.

The officiant joins the bride's right hand and the groom's right hand.

OFFICIANT: Now that _____ and _____ have given themselves to each other by solemn vows, with the joining of hands and the giving and receiving of rings, I pronounce that they are husband and wife, in the name of the Father, and the Son, and the Holy Spirit. Those whom God has joined together, let no one put asunder.

CONGREGATION: Amen.

The officiant directs the congregation to stand.

OFFICIANT: Let us stand and pray together the words our Savior taught us.

All stand and recite the Lord's Prayer.

Presbyterian

❧No. 1

OFFICIANT: Do you, _____, take _____ to be your wife/husband? Do you promise to love, honor, cherish and protect her/him, forsaking all others and holding only unto her/him?

BRIDE/GROOM: I do.

I, _____, take thee, _____, to be my wife/husband to have and to hold, in sickness and in health, for richer or for poorer, and I promise my love to you . . .

With this ring, I thee wed; all my love, I do thee give.

❧ No. 2

BRIDE/GROOM: I, _____, take thee, _____, to be my wedded husband/wife, and I do promise and covenant, before God and these witnesses, to be thy loving and faithful husband/wife; in plenty and in want, in joy and in sorrow, in sickness and in health, as long as we both shall live.

_____, this ring I give you, in token and pledge of our constant faith and abiding love.

Methodist

The Methodist religious vows (as well as Episcopal and Lutheran, which follow) specifically note the importance of taking the spouse "to live together after God's ordinance in the Holy Estate of matrimony." The exchange of rings in the Methodist ceremony also invokes the Holy Trinity, as seen in the second example.

■ EXAMPLES ■

❧ No. 1

BRIDE/GROOM: I, _____, ask you, _____, to be my husband/wife, as my friend and my love. On this day I affirm the relationship we have enjoyed, looking to the future to deepen and strengthen it. I will be yours in plenty and in want, in sickness and in health, in failure and in triumph. Together we will dream, will stumble but restore each other, we will share all things, serving each other and our fellow humanity. I will cherish and respect you, comfort and encourage you; be open with you, and stay with you as long as we both shall live, both freed and bound by our love.

In token and pledge of the vow between us made, with this ring I thee wed; in the name of the Father, and of the Son, and of the Holy Spirit. Amen.

No. 2

BRIDE/GROOM: I, _____, take thee, _____, to be my husband/wife, to have and to hold, from this day forward, for better, for worse, for richer for poorer, in sickness and in health, to love and to cherish, till death do us part, and thereto I pledge thee my faith.

United Methodist Church
Declaration of Intent

The declaration of intent in the United Methodist Church is often referred to as "the charge to the couple." It is a somewhat old-fashioned term that is used to make sure the couple is joining in marriage of their own free will. The declaration generally occurs early in the ceremony.

❧No. 1

OFFICIANT: Christ calls you into union with Him and with one another. I ask you now in the presence of God and this congregation to declare your intent. Will you have this man to be your husband, to live together in a holy marriage? Will you love him, comfort him, honor and keep him in sickness and in health, and forsaking all others, be faithful to him as long as you both shall live?

BRIDE: I will.

OFFICIANT: Will you have this woman to be your wife, to live together in a holy marriage? Will you love her, comfort her, honor and keep her in sickness and in health, and forsaking all others, be faithful to her as long as you both shall live?

GROOM: I will.

BRIDE/GROOM: I, _____, take you to be my wedded husband/wife, and I do promise and covenant, before God and these witnesses, to be your loving and faithful wife/husband, in plenty and in want, in joy and in sorrow, in sickness and in health, as long as we both shall live.

No. 2

BRIDE/GROOM: I take you, _____, to be my husband/wife from this day forward, to join with you and share all that is to come, and I promise to be faithful to you.

OFFICIANT: _____, you stand before God and this congregation to declare your intent. Will you have this man/woman to be your husband/wife, to live together in a holy marriage? Will you love him/her, comfort him/her, honor him/her, and keep him/her in sickness and in health, and forsaking all others, be faithful to him/her as long as you both shall live?

BRIDE/GROOM: I will.

Lutheran

■ EXAMPLES ■

No. 1

BRIDE/GROOM: I, _____, take you, _____, to be my husband/wife, and these things I promise you:

I will be faithful to you and honest with you;

I will respect, trust, help and care for you;

I will share my life with you;

I will forgive you as we have been forgiven; and I will try with you better to understand ourselves, the world, and God; through the

best and the worst of what is to come as long as we live.

No. 2

BRIDE/GROOM: I, _____, take you, _____, to be my husband/wife, and pledge thee my troth, so long as we both shall live.

No. 3

BRIDE/GROOM: _____, our miracle lies in the path we have chosen together. I enter into this marriage with you knowing that the true magic of love is not to avoid changes, but to navigate them successfully. Let us commit until death parts us.

Baptist

■ EXAMPLE ■

I, _____, take thee, _____, to be my husband/wife, and before God and these witnesses I promise to be a faithful and true (husband/wife).

Unitarian-Universalist

There is most often no set service in this religion; the vows are designed by the officiant together with the couple. However, these are two typical Unitarian-Universalist wedding vow phrasings:

❧ No. 1

OFFICIANT: _____, will you take _____ to be your husband/wife; to love, honor, and cherish him/her now and forevermore?

BRIDE/GROOM: I will.

❧ No. 2

BRIDE/GROOM: I, _____, take you, _____, to be my husband/wife; to have and to hold from this day forward, for better, for worse, for richer, for poorer, in sickness and in health, to love and cherish always.

❧ No. 3

OFFICIANT: _____, will you have _____ to be your husband/wife, to live together in creating an abiding marriage? Will you love and honor, comfort and cherish him/her in sickness and in health, in sorrow and in joy, from this day forward?

United Church of Christ
■ EXAMPLE ■

BRIDE/GROOM: I, _____, take you, _____, to be my husband/wife, and I promise to love and sustain you in the bonds of marriage from this day forward, in sickness and in health, in plenty and in want, in joy and in sorrow, till death shall part us, according to God's holy ordinance.

Quaker

■ EXAMPLE ■

❧ No. 1

In the presence of God and these our Friends, I,_____, take thee to be my husband/wife, promising with Divine assistance to be unto thee a loving and faithful husband/wife as long as we both shall live.

❧ No. 2

On this the [day of month] in the year of our Lord, [year] A.D., _____ and _____, appeared together, and [husband's name], taking [wife's name] by the hand, did, on this solemn and joyous occasion, declare that he took _____ to be his wife, promising with Divine assistance to be unto her a loving and faithful husband; and then, in the same assembly, [wife's name] did in like manner declare that she took _____ to be her husband, promising with Divine assistance to be unto him a loving and faithful wife. And moreover they, _____ and _____, did, as further confirmation thereof, then and there, to this certificate set their hands. And we, having been present at the marriage, have as witnesses hereunto set our hands to this certificate.

Nondenominational Protestant

Some Protestant churches are not formally affiliated with specific denominations. Following are two examples of traditional nondenominational vows.

■ EXAMPLES ■

❧No. 1

OFFICIANT: Will you have this woman/man to be your wedded wife/husband, to live together in holy matrimony? Will you love her/him, comfort her/him, honor and keep her/him in sickness and in health, in sorrow and in joy, and forsaking all others, be faithful to her/him as long as you both shall live?

BRIDE/GROOM: I do.

OFFICIANT: This celebration is an outward token of a sacred and inward union of the hearts which the church does bless and the state makes legal — a union created by loving purpose and kept by abiding will. Is it in this spirit and for this purpose that you have come here to be joined together?

BRIDE/GROOM: Yes, I have.

The couple says the vows from memory or repeats after the officiant.

BRIDE/GROOM: I take you to be my wedded wife/husband, to have and to hold from this day forward, for better, for worse, for richer, for poorer, in sickness and in health, to love and to cherish, till death do us part. This is my solemn vow. According to God's holy ordinance; and thereto I plight you my troth.

❧No. 2

OFFICIANT TO THE GROOM: _____, wilt thou have _____ to be thy wedded wife, to live together after God's ordinance, in the holy estate of matrimony? Wilt thou love her, comfort her, honor and keep her, in sickness and in health; and forsaking all others, keep thee only unto her, so long as ye both shall live?

GROOM: I will.

OFFICIANT TO THE BRIDE: _____, wilt thou have _____ to be thy wedded husband, to live together after God's ordinance, in the holy estate of matrimony? Wilt thou obey him, and serve him, love, honor and keep him, in sickness and in health, and forsaking all others, keep thee only unto him, so long as ye both shall live?

BRIDE: I will.

Traditional Anglican Vows

Like many traditional wedding vows, the origin of the vows used in Anglican services can be traced back to the *Book of Common Prayer*. Although this customary wedding promise includes the woman pledging to "love, cherish, and obey" her husband, the Church of England has, in many cases, dropped the "obey" and replaced it with "protect." The church urges its ministers to emphasize to couples preparing for marriage that men and women are of equal value in the eyes of God.

The bride and groom proceed to the area where the marriage will take place. They face each other and, at this stage, don't usually hold hands.

OFFICIANT: We have come together here in the sight of God, and in the presence of this congregation, to join together this man and this woman in holy matrimony; which is an honorable state of life, instituted from the beginning by God himself, signifying to us the spiritual union that is possible between

Christ and those who reach out to him. Christ adorned and beautified matrimony with his presence and with the first sign by which he revealed his glory, at the marriage in Cana of Galilee; and holy scriptures commands that all should hold it in honor. It is therefore not to be entered upon unadvisedly, lightly, or merely to satisfy physical desires; but prayerfully, with careful thought, and with reverence for God, duly considering the purposes for which it was ordained. It was ordained for the procreation of children and that they might be brought up in the nurture and instruction of the Lord, to the praise of his holy name. It was ordained so that those to whom God has granted the gift of marriage might live a chaste and holy life, as befits members of God's beautiful creation. And it was ordained for the mutual companionship, help, and comfort that the one ought to have of the other, both in prosperity and adversity.

Into this holy manner of life, _____ and _____ come now to be joined. Therefore if anyone can show any just cause why they may not be joined together, let them speak now or hereafter remain silent.

I charge you both, as you will answer before God, who is the judge of all and from whom no secrets are hidden, that if either of you know any reason why you may not lawfully be joined together in matrimony, you now confess it. For be assured that those who marry otherwise than God's word allows are not joined together by God, neither is their matrimony lawful in his sight.

OFFICIANT TO GROOM: _____, will you have _____ as your wife, to live together, as God has ordained, in the holy state of matrimony? Will you love her, cherish her, honor and protect her, in sickness and in health; and, forsaking all others, be faithful to her, as long as you both shall live?

GROOM: I will

OFFICIANT TO BRIDE: _____, will you have _____ as your husband, to live together, as God has ordained, in the holy state of matrimony? Will you love him, cherish him, honor and protect him, in sickness and in health; and, forsaking all others, be faithful to him, as long as you both shall live?

BRIDE: I will ·

OFFICIANT: Who brings this woman to be married to this man?

FAMILY MEMBER: I do

OFFICIANT: Members of the families of _____ and _____, do you give your blessing to this marriage?

FAMILY MEMBERS: We do

The bride and groom face each other and repeat.

GROOM: I _____ take you _____ to be my wife, according to God's holy ordinance: to have and to hold from this day forward, for better for worse, for richer for poorer, in sickness and in health, to love and to cherish, until we are parted by death. And to this I pledge you my word.

BRIDE: I _____ take you _____ to be my husband, according to God's holy ordinance: to have and to hold from this day forward, for better for worse, for richer for poorer, in sickness and in health, to love and to cherish, until we are parted by death. And to this I pledge you my word.

The Groom gives his ring to the Bride, then the Bride gives her ring to the Groom. They each repeat:

With this ring I wed you, with my body I worship you; with all that I am and all that I have I honor you: in the name of the Father, and of the Son, and of the Holy Spirit. Amen.

The couple face the front, and holding hands, bow their heads.

OFFICIANT: Let us pray. Eternal God, preserver of all mankind, giver of all spiritual grace and author of everlasting life: send your blessing upon this man and this woman whom we bless in your name; that as Isaac and Rebecca lived faithfully together, so _____ and _____ may surely perform and keep the vow and covenant made between them, of which this ring given and received is a token and pledge, and may ever remain in perfect love and peace together, and live according to your laws; through Jesus Christ our Lord. Amen.

Those whom God has joined together let not man put asunder.

_____ and _____ have now witnessed to their mutual consent before God and this company; they have pledged their solemn word to each other; and they have confirmed it by the giving and receiving of a ring and by the joining of hands. I therefore declare them to be husband and wife: in the name of the Father, and of the Son, and of the Holy Spirit. Amen.

God the Father, God the Son, God the Holy Spirit, bless, preserve, and keep you; the Lord mercifully with his favor look upon you and fill you with all spiritual blessing and grace, that you may so live together in this life, that in the world to come you may have life everlasting. Amen.

The bride and groom may kiss at this point.

OFFICIANT RECITES THE CLOSING PRAYER: Almighty God, who by joining man and woman together taught us from the beginning that we should not separate what you have joined as one; we praise you that you have consecrated the state of matrimony to such an excellent purpose that in it is signified the spiritual marriage and unity between Christ and those who reach out to him. Look mercifully on these your servants that this man may love his wife, according to your word, as Christ loved broken humanity, and gave himself up for us, cherishing us as himself; and also that this woman may be loving and generous, responsive and faithful to her husband. O Lord, bless them both, and grant them to inherit your everlasting kingdom; through Jesus Christ our Lord. Amen.

God the Father enrich you with his grace, God the Son make you holy in his love, God the Holy Spirit strengthen you with his joy. The Lord bless you and keep you in eternal life. Amen.

Episcopal

❦ No. 1

BRIDE/GROOM: I, _____, take thee, _____, to be my wedded husband/wife, to have and to hold from this day forward, for better for worse, for richer or for poorer, in sickness and in health, to love and to cherish, 'til death do us part, according to God's ordinance; and thereto I pledge thee my troth.

❦ No. 2

BRIDE/GROOM: I, _____, vow to be your faithful husband/wife, understanding that marriage is a lifelong union, and not to be entered into lightly, for the purpose of mutual fellowship, encouragement and understanding; for the procreation of children and their physical and spiritual nurture. I hereby give myself to you in this cause, with my sacred vow before God.

❦ No. 3

BRIDE/GROOM: In the Name of God, I, _____, take you, _____, to be my husband/wife, to have and to hold from this day forward, for better or worse, for richer or poorer, in sickness and in health, to love and to cherish, until we are parted by death. This is my solemn vow.

Traditional Orthodox Vows

In the United States, the Orthodox Church is known by many names: the Eastern Orthodox Church, the Russian Orthodox Church, Greek Orthodox, Syrian Orthodox, Serbian Orthodox, Romanian Orthodox, etc. They are, in fact, all names for one and the same church with one and the same faith and practice. Within these churches, of course, there are cultural differences which do not necessarily differ from the essence of the faith.

Orthodox Christians tend to be philosophical, abstract, and mystical in their thinking. Their views on subjects such as the use of images (icons), the nature of the Holy Spirit, and the date on which Easter should be celebrated differ from Western approaches which tend to be based in pragmatism. The wedding vows reflect this belief system.

Eastern Orthodox

In both Greek and Russian Orthodox churches, wedding vows are conducted silently. The ceremony is quite long and almost always includes the exchange of rings. The bride and the groom exchange rings three times to symbolize the Holy Trinity. The ceremony also includes the crowning, at which time the bride and groom receive crowns. When the priest removes the crowns from their heads he recites a blessing: "Be though magnified, O bridegroom." The couple is at that moment married.

Carpatho-Russian Orthodox

■ EXAMPLE ■

Although vows at most Eastern Orthodox marriage ceremonies are silent rituals, in the Carpatho-Russian sect the bride and groom do speak their vows aloud.

BRIDE/GROOM: I,_____, take you, _____, as my wedded wife/husband and I promise to love, honor and respect; to be faithful to you, and not to forsake you until death do us part. So help me God, one in the Holy Trinity, and all the Saints.

TRADITIONAL JEWISH VOWS

In the Jewish wedding tradition, the exchange of vows is not as critical a part of the marriage ceremony as it is in other faiths. What binds a man and woman together in matrimony is their faith and the holiness of the event. According to Jewish law, very little is required in the way of official ceremonies, and the service doesn't even necessitate the presence of a rabbi or other clergy at the wedding. Rather, halachah — the body of Jewish law that supplements scriptural law and forms the legal part of the Talmud — requires only that two witnesses who meet certain criteria be present. However, this does not mean that vows are not written and presented aloud before the guests.

The wedding ceremony often takes place outdoors under a canopy called a chuppah, and it is customary for the bride and groom to stand beneath it during the service. Traditionally made of cloth, the chuppah is held up by four poles that symbolize the home the couple will build together. It is a wonderful custom to be married under the open sky as the act proclaims that "our home is subject to nature" and stresses the couple's faith in God's protection.

The ketubah is a marriage contract that details the marriage responsibilities of the husband to his wife. It is signed by the groom, as well as two witnesses, and given to the bride during the wedding ceremony. Ketubot (plural of ketubah) can be as plain or as adorned as the couple decides. Many choose to have one commissioned by an artist or calligrapher and hang it proudly in their new home as a reminder of the vows they made to each other. The wedding Ketubah is a part of all branches of Judaism: Reform, Conservative, and Orthodox.

Orthodox Jewish Weddings have several different traditions and laws from the other branches. The exchange of rings, for example, requires the wedding band to be solid all the way around; i.e. a full circle; it does not necessarily have to be gold.

The ring also has to be the property of the groom. During the service, an Orthodox rabbi may ask "Do you own this ring?" The context of that question is because the ring is presented to the bride as an item of value (part of the dowry) and it is part of the marriage contract.

The breaking of the glass at the end of the ceremony is an important element of the Jewish wedding. It serves to remind the bride, groom, and everyone in attendance that marriage should be considered an irrevocable act as permanent as the breaking of the glass. The breaking of the glass is also a reminder of the weakness of a marriage, indicating that sometimes a single thoughtless act, breach of trust, or infidelity can damage a marriage and is often hard to undo (hence the broken glass, which cannot be put back together).

In a Conservative Jewish wedding ceremony, vows from the Rabbinical Assembly Manual might be used. These are shown in the first example. In a Reform Jewish ceremony, the rabbi might say the question-and-answer vows as in the second example.

Conservative
■ EXAMPLE ■

RABBI, TO THE GROOM: Do you, _____, take _____ to be your lawful wedded wife, to love, to honor, and to cherish?

GROOM: I do.

RABBI, TO THE BRIDE: Do you, _____, take _____ to be your lawful wedded husband, to love, to honor, and to cherish?

BRIDE: I do.

RABBI, TO THE GROOM: Do you, _____, put this ring upon the finger of your bride and say to her: "Be thou consecrated to me, as my wife, by this ring, according to the Law of Moses and of Israel?"

RABBI ASKS THE BRIDE TO REPEAT: May this ring I receive from thee be a token of my having become thy wife according to the Law of Moses and of Israel.

IN A DOUBLE RING CEREMONY, THE BRIDE SAYS: This ring is a symbol that thou art my husband in accordance with the Law of Moses and Israel.

Reform
■ EXAMPLES ■

No. 1

OFFICIANT, TO THE GROOM: Do you _____, take _____ to be your wife?

GROOM: I do.

OFFICIANT: Do you promise to love, cherish and protect her, whether in good fortune or in adversity, and to seek with her a life hallowed by the faith of Israel?

GROOM: I do.

OFFICIANT, TO THE BRIDE: Do you _____, take _____ to be your husband?

BRIDE: I do.

OFFICIANT: Do you promise to love, cherish and protect him, whether in good fortune or in adversity, and to seek with him a life hallowed by the faith of Israel?

BRIDE: I do

OFFICIANT, TO THE GROOM: _____, as you place this ring upon the finger of _____, speak to her these vows:

With this ring be thou consecrated unto me as my wife according to the law of God and the faith of Israel."

OFFICIANT, TO THE BRIDE: _____, as you place this ring upon the finger of _____, speak to him these vows:

With this ring be thou consecrated unto me as my husband according to the law of God and the faith of Israel.

❧No. 2

RABBI: O God, supremely blessed, supreme in might and glory, guide and bless this groom and bride. Standing here in the presence of God, the Guardian of the home, ready to enter into the bond of wedlock, answer in the fear of God, and in the hearing of those assembled: Do you, _____, of your own free will and consent take _____ to be your wife/husband and do you promise to love, honor, and cherish her/him throughout life?

BRIDE/GROOM: I do.

Traditional Ethnic Vows & Rituals

The traditions of ethnic cultures from around the world are increasingly found in our daily lives. They are a testament to the blending of societies that we all find in the world in which we live. These lively and time-honored customs are everywhere we look, but most especially they are seen in ceremonies and rituals like weddings.

For instance, there's a good chance many are familiar with the following — thought to have originated with the English Victorians: Something old, something new, something borrowed, something blue . . . According to tradition, the "old" should be something that once belonged to a happily married woman; this will assure the new bride happiness in her union. The 'new" is the wedding outfit: the gown, shoes, headpiece, etc. and symbolizes the new, fresh start she undertakes. The "borrowed" is generally something made of gold, often a ring, brooch, or necklace that guarantees wealth and good fortune. The "blue" is a symbol of the heavens above and of true love the couple will find with each other.

Why the ring finger of the left hand for a Christian ring ceremony? This tradition is passed down from the Romans because they believed that is the best way to protect the valuable ring. Their reasoning? The left hand is used less often than the right.

In the Jewish tradition, joyous and life affirming wedding music and dance has imbued many an American ceremony with unbridled delight.

Ethnic wedding vows and ceremonies can provide a link to one's heritage as well as an infusion of enthusiasm.

African-American
Broom Jumping

Broom jumping is a wonderful tradition that dates back many years. A decorated broom can be bought from a speciality store, or the couple can simply use a household broom; the type doesn't matter, nor does the size of the broom. Often couples will decorate their own broom using the colors they have chosen for the wedding.

Bridesmaids often help the bride decorate the broom, but another option is to supply wedding guests with ribbons and give everyone the chance to tie ribbons around the broom before the ceremony. This participation by all the wedding guests is in keeping with the African tradition of community involvement.

To begin the ceremony, the host will ask all the family members and friends to make a circle around the couple as they stand in front of the broom on the floor.

■ EXAMPLE ■

OFFICIANT: Let us give our support to this new family that is formed by the joining and the combining of two families, and we ask their community to support the couple.

As Mr. & Mrs. _____ jump this broom, let them look forward to a new life and home together as husband and wife.

The jumping of the broom is a symbol of sweeping away the old and welcoming the new, or a symbol of a new beginning.

Would everyone count 1, 2, 3 . . . jump!

Native American
Blessing of the Apaches
■ EXAMPLE ■

OFFICIANT: Now you will feel no rain, for each of you will be shelter for the other. Now you will feel no cold, for each of you will be warmth to the other. Now there will be no loneliness, for each of you will be companion to the other. Now you are two persons, but there is only one life before you. May beauty surround you both in the journey ahead and through all the years; may happiness be your companion and your days together be good and long upon the earth. Treat yourselves and each other with respect, and remind yourselves often of what brought you together. Give the highest priority to the tenderness, gentleness, and kindness that your connection deserves. When frustration, difficulty; and fear assail your relationship — as they threaten all relationships at one time or another — remember to focus on what is right between you, not only the part which seems wrong. In this way, you can ride out the storms when clouds hide the face of the sun in your lives — remembering that even if you lose sight of it for a moment, the sun is still there. And if each of you takes responsibility for the quality of your life together, it will be marked by abundance and delight.

Cherokee Prayer

■ EXAMPLE ■

OFFICIANT: God in heaven above, please protect the ones we love. We honor all you created as we pledge our hearts and lives together. We honor mother-earth — and ask for our marriage to be abundant and grow stronger through the seasons; we honor fire — and ask that our union be warm and glowing with love in our hearts; we honor wind — and ask that we sail though life safe and calm as in our father's arms; we honor water — to clean and soothe our relationship — that it may never thirst for love; with all the forces of the universe you created, we pray for harmony and true happiness as we forever grow young together. Amen.

Eskimo Love Song

■ EXAMPLE ■

BRIDE/GROOM: You are my husband/wife. My feet shall run because of you; my feet dance because of you; my heart shall beat because of you; my eyes see because of you; my mind thinks because of you. And I shall love because of you.

Irish

There are many traditional Irish wedding vows, ceremonies, and verses; one might add the perfect touch of ethnicity to your wedding day. A basic vow might include these simple words:

BRIDE/GROOM: I, _____, now take you, _____, to be my husband/wife. In the presence of God and before these witnesses I promise to be a loving, faithful, and loyal husband/wife to you, for as long as we both shall live.

A much older traditional vow used in Irish church weddings expresses similar sentiments:

BRIDE/GROOM: By the power that Christ brought from heaven, mayst thou love me. As the sun follows its course, mayst thou follow me. As light to the eye, as bread to the hungry, as joy to the heart, may thy presence be with me, oh one that I love, 'til death comes to part us asunder.

One lasting symbol of the Irish marriage is the Claddagh wedding ring, a traditional ring that symbolizes love, friendship, and loyalty. When the exchange of vows includes an exchange of rings, this ring is the traditional choice.

The circular band forms two hands holding a heart with a crown on top. The ring is given with the Phrase of the Claddagh:

BRIDE/GROOM: With these hands I give you my heart, and crown it with my love.

Following are other examples of Irish traditions that you might incorporate into your ceremony.

Vow of Unity
■ EXAMPLE ■

BRIDE/GROOM: We swear by peace and love to stand, heart to heart and hand in hand. Mark, O Spirit, and hear us now, confirming this, our Sacred Vow.

Loving Cup Ceremony
■ EXAMPLE ■

This ceremony takes place as the couple sips the sacramental wine during the exchange of vows. The officiant recites these words:

OFFICIANT: And now please drink to the love you've shared in the past.

The couple sip from the cup.

OFFICIANT: Drink to your love in the present, on this your wedding day.

The couple sip from the cup, again.

OFFICIANT: And drink to your love in the future and forever more.

The couple take a final sip from the cup.

Traditional Blessing

May the road rise to meet you,

May the wind be always at your back.

May the sun shine warm upon your face,

The rains fall soft upon your fields.

And until we meet again,

May God hold you in the palm of His hand.

May God be with you and bless you;

May you see your children's children.

May you be poor in misfortune,

Rich in blessings,

May you know nothing but happiness

From this day forward.

May the road rise to meet you

May the wind be always at your back

May the warm rays of sun fall upon your home

And may the hand of a friend always be near.

May green be the grass you walk on,

May blue be the skies above you,

May pure be the joys that surround you,

May true be the hearts that love you.

Celtic

The Celts are descended from groups that lived primarily in northwestern Europe. Their rich history of words and music often provides a bounty of ceremonial traditions. Below is one of the more customary Celtic wedding vows.

■ EXAMPLE ■

BRIDE/GROOM: I vow to you the first cut of my meat, the first sip of my wine, from this day on it shall be only your name I cry out in the night and into your eyes that I smile each morning; I shall be a shield for your back as you are for mine, nor shall a grievous word be spoken about us, for our marriage is sacred between us and no stranger shall hear my grievance. Above and beyond this, I will cherish and honor you through this life and into the next.

Ye are Blood of my Blood, and Bone of my Bone. I give ye my Body, that we Two might be One. I give ye my Spirit, 'til our Life shall be Done.

You cannot possess me for I belong to myself, but while we both wish it, I give you that which is mine to give. You cannot command me for I am a free person But I shall serve you in those ways you require, and the honeycomb will taste sweeter coming from my hand.

Hindu Vows

Hindu wedding vows are quite strict. The ceremony, known as a Samskara, has many parts that are thousands of years old and include chanting, Sanskrit blessings, and ritual. The wedding can last for days or weeks, but in the West usually is complete in about two hours.

Normally a Hindu priest (pandit) takes the couple and their families through the sacrament of marriage. One very important part of the Hindu ceremony is the lighting of a sacred fire. This fire is created from ghee and woolen wicks and invokes the god Agni (fire) to bear witness to the ceremony. (Fire is very important in the Hindu faith as it is considered a purifier with the ability to sustain life.) After the bride and groom are seated in front of the holy fire (agni), the priest recites various mantras. In yet another ritual called mangalfera, the bride and groom walk around the fire four times (each a symbol of the four ashrams of life), praying and exchanging vows of duty, love, fidelity, and respect. The priest directs family members to make offerings into the fire.

Following this is the highlight of the ceremony, called Saptapadi or the Seven Steps. At this point it is traditional for the bride's sari to be tied to the groom's kurta, or a sari shawl can be draped from his shoulder to her sari. The groom then leads the bride by her little finger linked with his and they walk seven steps around the fire while the officiant chants seven vows for the strength of the marriage. As the couple walk around the fire they are in essence agreeing to these vows. As they take each step they throw small bits of puffed rice into the fire, which is representative of their new life together.

The Seven Steps

- Let us take the first step vowing to provide for our household a nourishing and pure diet, avoiding those foods injurious to healthy living.

- Let us take the second step vowing to develop physical, mental and spiritual powers.

- Let us take the third step vowing to increase our wealth by righteous means and proper use.

- Let us take the fourth step vowing to acquire knowledge, happiness, and harmony by mutual love and trust.

- Let us take the fifth step, so that we be blessed with strong, virtuous, and heroic children.

- Let us take the sixth step for self-restraint and longevity.

- Finally, let us take the seventh step and be true companions and remain lifelong partners by this wedlock.

After the seventh step, the groom speaks to the bride about their friendship and partnership. Once the seven steps are completed, the couple is pronounced husband and wife.

Muslim Vows

The only real requirement for a Muslim wedding is that it include the signing of a marriage contract. In fact, depending on the culture, Islamic sect, and observance of the gender separation rules, Muslim marriage traditions differ greatly. Marriages are usually not held in mosques, and men and women are separated during the ceremony and reception. Islam actually authorizes no official clergy, so any Muslim who understands Islamic tradition can be the official for the wedding. If a Muslim wedding is held in a mosque, however, then a marriage officer (known as a qazi or madhun) may preside over the wedding.

The marriage contract, called a meher, is a formal statement identifying the financial amount the groom will give the bride. There are two parts to the meher: an amount due before the marriage is consummated and an amount given to the bride during her lifetime. Nowadays many Muslim couples use the ring as the amount due before the marriage, and the groom gives it to the bride at the ceremony.

The amount of money given later can be a small amount; it is really a formality. In some cases there might be a gift of money, land, jewelry, or something else of value. The gift belongs to the bride and she can do with it what she wants unless the marriage ends before consummation.

The marriage contract is signed during the first part of the ceremony, called the nikah. In this ceremony the groom or someone standing in for him proposes to the bride in front of at least two people and also discusses the details of the marriage contract. The bride and groom show their free will by saying the word qabul, which means "I accept" in Arabic, three times. Following this the bride and groom sign the contract along with two male witnesses. The marriage is then considered legal by both civil and religious law.

After the contract is signed, it is customary for the bride and groom to share a piece of sweet fruit. If the bride and groom have been separated during the ceremony, then a male representative (wali) will act on the bride's behalf.

Sometimes an official adds something extra to the ceremony, but this would be after the nikah. During the nikah a recitation of the Fatihah (first chapter of the Koran) and blessings also take place.

As a rule there are no vows in a Muslim ceremony. Rather, the official talks to the bride and groom about the meaning of marriage and the responsibilities that it entails to one another and to Allah.

However, sometimes tradition is broken and the Muslim couple do choose to have vows. Two possible recitations follow.

■ EXAMPLES ■

❧ No. 1

BRIDE/GROOM: I, _____, take you, _____, to be my husband/wife. I promise to be true to you in good times and in bad, in sickness and in health. I will love you and honor you all the days of my life.

BRIDE: I pledge, in honesty and sincerity, to be for you an obedient and faithful wife.

GROOM: I pledge, in honesty and sincerity, to be for you an obedient and faithful husband.

❧ No. 2

BRIDE: I, _____, offer you myself in marriage in accordance with the instructions of the Holy Koran and the Holy Prophet, peace and blessing be upon him. I pledge, in honesty and with sincerity, to be for you an obedient and faithful wife.

GROOM: I pledge, in honesty and sincerity, to be for you a faithful and helpful husband.

Buddhist Ceremony

In the Buddhist tradition, the day of the wedding begins at a temple, where the couple individually will ask for a blessing from Buddha. Afterward the bride and groom are dressed in traditional outfits that depict the particular region of the country they are from.

The chosen wedding time is often determined by the auspiciousness of the stars. At the appointed time, the bride and groom are taken to their own shrine room, seeing one another for the first time that day.

Buddhist weddings do not require monks or the use of a temple's shrine room. However, it is important that there be a shrine to Buddha with candles, flowers, incense, and a statue or image of Buddha wherever the ceremony does take place.

The ceremony actually begins as everyone recites the Vandana, Tisarana, and Pancasila readings. The couple lights the candles and incense sticks surrounding Buddha's image and offers him the flowers in the shrine.

There are no vows in a Buddhist wedding, but the bride and groom do recite their probable deeds using the "Sigolovda Sutta" as the guide. If monks are in attendance there will be chanting both before and after this recitation. The bride and groom can also exchange rings if they choose.

■ EXAMPLE ■

BRIDE/GROOM: _____, in the future, happy occasions will come as surely as the morning. Difficult times will come as surely as the night. When things go joyously, meditate according to the Buddhist tradition. When things go badly, meditate. Meditation in the manner of the Compassionate Buddha will guide your life. To say the words *love* and *compassion* is easy. But to accept that love and compassion are built upon patience and perseverance is not easy.

If, as a couple, you are interested in breaking away from the boundaries of traditional ceremonies and vows, this part of the book may appeal to you.

Nontraditional vows are often popular with ceremonies that do not take place in conventional locations; those that include children or spouses from previous marriages; or a second or third marriage. The vows and ceremonies included on the following pages offer the opportunity to be more creative in your declarations to your spouse-to-be.

The section begins with a standard civil ceremony, then offers helpful vow options for particular situations from mixing religions and cultures to blending families. You'll find interesting and meaningful vows and rituals to include in your ceremony, as well as information on renewing your vows and writing your own vows.

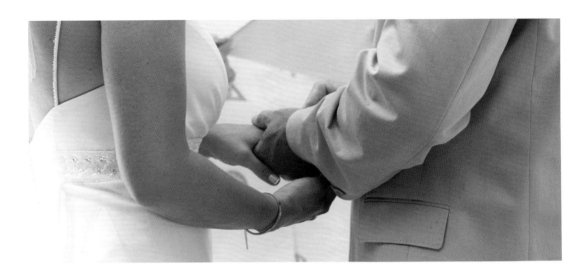

Civil Ceremonies

A civil ceremony is an option for any couple that does not wish to include religious aspects in their ceremony or wishes to determine exactly where the ceremony will take place and what goes into the service. Because there is no set religious aspect in a basic civil ceremony, a couple is free to include any special readings, vows, or rituals that they choose. A civil ceremony may take place anywhere from the registrar's office or a judge's chambers to a friend's backyard or an exotic seaside resort. Be sure to check the laws of the state in which you plan to get married to determine who is considered a legal officiate.

Because there are no set limitations on the ceremony itself, the civil ceremony becomes a build-your-own ceremony. Review the vows, quotes, and rituals throughout this book to help you piece together the ceremony that is just right for you. The following is a very simple civil vow that you can use on its own or to begin to shape your final vow.

_____, I take you to be my lawfully wedded husband/wife. Before these witnesses I vow to love you and care for you as long as we both shall live. I take you, with all your faults and your strengths, as I offer myself to you with my faults and my strengths. I will help you when you need help, and will turn to you when I need help. I choose you as the person with whom I will spend my life.

Interfaith and Intercultural Vows

Each year, more than 40,000 couples enter into interfaith marriages. These marriages offer a wonderful opportunity to join two faiths or cultures. These marriages often present a challenge to plan a wedding ceremony that will reflect the bride and groom's differing religious backgrounds, traditions, and beliefs and also be sensitive to the beliefs and traditions of their parents, other relatives, and guests.

Interfaith

■ EXAMPLE ■

❧ No. 1

> I, _____, take you, to be my wife/husband. I promise to be true to you in good times and in bad, in sickness and in health. I will love and honor you all the days of my life.

❧ No. 2

> _____, I have enjoyed the time we've spent talking about what our different faiths mean to us. We have discovered much that we share in common. It is my prayer that the candles we have lit together today in unity will enlighten our path to the future. I promise to honor your traditions as I honor you.

> I, _____, take you, _____, to be my wedded husband/wife; and I promise and covenant, before God and these witnesses, to be your loving and faithful husband/wife, in plenty and in want, in joy and in sorrow, in sickness and in health, as long as we both shall live.

Interfaith Jewish Vows

■ EXAMPLE ■

OFFICIANT: We are gathered here today to celebrate one of life's greatest moments, to give recognition to the worth and beauty of love, and to add our best wishes to the words which shall unite _____ and _____ in marriage.

Who is it that brings this woman forward to this man?

PARENT OR FAMILY: [respond dependent on who is escorting the bride.]

OFFICIANT: _____ and _____, life is given to each of us as individuals, and yet we must learn to live together. Love is given to us by our family and friends — we learn to love by being loved. Learning to love and living together is one of the greatest challenges of life; and it is the shared goal of a married life. But we also must remember that it is not mankind that created love, but God who created love. Blessed art thou, O Lord God, creator of all things.

OFFICIANT TO GROOM: Do you _____, take _____ to be your wife?

GROOM: I do.

OFFICIANT: Do you promise to love, cherish, and protect her, whether in good fortune or in adversity, and to seek with her a life hallowed by the faith of Israel?

GROOM: I do.

OFFICIANT TO BRIDE: Do you _____, take _____ to be your husband?

BRIDE: I do.

OFFICIANT: Do you promise to love, cherish and protect him, whether in good fortune or in adversity, and to seek with him a life hallowed by the faith of Israel?

BRIDE: I do.

The Blessing

OFFICIANT: May the bride and groom now receive the benediction:

Blessed art thou O Lord God, Ruler of the Universe, creator of man.

Blessed art thou O Lord God, Ruler of the Universe, who hast fashioned us in thine own image and who established marriage for the fulfillment and perpetuation of life in accordance with thy holy purpose. Blessed art thou O Lord God, creator of man.

Blessed art thou O Lord God, ruler of the universe, who art the source of all gladness and joy. Through thy grace we attain affection, companionship, love, and peace. Grant that the love that unites this man and this woman grow in abiding happiness. May their family be ennobled through their devotion to the faith of Israel. May there be peace in their home, quietness and confidence in their hearts. May they be sustained by thy comforting presence in the midst of our people and thy promise of salvation for all mankind.

Blessed art thou O Lord God, Ruler of the Universe, who dost unite this man and this woman in the holy joy of matrimony. Amen.

Wine Ritual
(If wine is presented to the Bridegroom and his Bride.)

OFFICIANT: As you have shared the wine from this cup, so may you, under God's guidance, draw contentment, comfort, and strength from the cup of life. May you find life's joys heightened, its bitterness sweetened, and all things hallowed by true companionship and love.

Exchange of Rings

OFFICIANT TO THE GROOM: _____, as you place this ring upon the finger of _____, speak to her these vows: With this ring, be thou consecrated unto me as my wife according to the law of God and the faith of Israel.

OFFICIANT TO THE BRIDE: _____, as you place this ring upon the finger of _____, speak to him these vows: With this ring, be thou consecrated unto me as my husband according to the law of God and the faith of Israel.

Charge to the Couple

OFFICIANT: _____ and _____, as the two of you come into this marriage uniting you as husband and wife, and as you this day affirm your faith and love for one another, I would ask that you always remember to cherish each other as special and unique individuals, that you respect the thoughts, ideas, and

suggestions of one another. Be able to forgive, do not hold grudges, and live each day that you may share it together — as from this day forward you shall be each other's home, comfort, and refuge, your marriage strengthened by your love and respect for each other.

If your ceremony will be a mixed faith marriage, an alternative Charge to the Couple may appeal as it emphasizes the power of the faith of each person — as opposed to submission to the faith — is where true respect is found.

Alternative Charge to the Couple

Just as two threads woven in opposite directions form a most beautiful tapestry, so too can your two lives merge together make a beautiful marriage. To make your relationship work will take love. This is the core of your marriage and why you are here today. It will take trust; to know in your hearts that you truly want the best for each other. It will take dedication; to stay open to one another and to learn and grow together. It will take faith; to go forward together without knowing exactly what the future brings. And it will take commitment; to hold true to the journey you both pledge today to share together.

Intercultural Vow

_____, our love has opened windows to the worlds we lived in as children. I have found profound respect for your heritage; but I am not part of it. We have vowed to live our adult lives together. Our marriage will be a new creation.

Now I promise to build bridges of understanding, and share the best of myself with your family, your friends, and you.

_____, with these rings we unite our hearts in tenderness and devotion. We will honor each other's cultures as we join customs to form a trusting relationship. We will protect, support, and encourage each other through life's joys and sorrows as we create a loving future. We promise to establish a home for ourselves and our children shaped by our respective heritages; a loving environment dedicated to peace, hope, and respect for all people. From this day forward our lives will be intertwined forever, blessed in faith, filled with compassion, understanding and love.

Handfasting

Handfasting, a forerunner of the modern-day wedding ceremony, dates back to the Celts. The practice began because in many rural villages during the Middle Ages, there was no priest or minister to perform an official marriage. In this case a couple would perform a temporary "marriage" that would last a year and a day, which was enough time for an official to come to town for the legal ceremony. A handfasting ceremony in itself is not recognized as legally binding, but depending on the state you live in and the person conducting the ceremony, it can be legally sanctioned when an official signs the marriage license. These days, handfasting rituals are often incorporated into contemporary weddings, whether religious or not, for the symbolism and tradition they add to the ceremony.

There are numerous handfasting ceremonies, from the pagan rituals to the Irish tradition in which the hands of the couple are bound together in a tartan cloth or cord and the wedding vows are exchanged. After that ceremony, the groom pins the tartan cloth to the bride's shoulder to signify that she is now a member of his family.

Regardless of the specific tradition, the ritual usually does include the symbolic and literal binding of the couple's hands with some sort of cord, which is the "hand fastening."

The term "to tie the knot" also comes from the handfasting ceremony.

Like most weddings, handfasting is usually done in front of friends and family. However, the couple can also hold a ceremony with no witness other than the officiate representing the couple's belief system. The symbolism is the most important thing. The couple make no lifelong promises to one another in this ceremony; rather, they make a commitment for a year and a day.

The ceremony usually involves a cleansing ritual to create a sacred space, and an invocation of the four elements (earth/air/fire/water) or directions (north/south/east/west). These elements of Nature are invited to witness and protect the couple as they make their way into the world as one. A priest or priestess performs the ceremony by lightly binding the hands of the couple together and speaking to them and the witnesses of the meaning of the ceremony. The couple then speak words of love and commitment to each other.

Following this the couple jump over a sword and broom while holding hands. The sword is symbolic of cutting ties with the old life, before they were together, and the broom represents sweeping away the remnants of their separate lives.

For pagans the most popular day for a handfasting ceremony is Beltane in May, which celebrates spring and the renewal of life. Samhain (the forerunner to Halloween) is the pagan and Wiccan New Year, and therefore is also considered an auspicious date.

Pagan Handfasting

OFFICIATE: We have come together here in celebration of the joining together of _____ and _____. There are many things to say about marriage. Much wisdom concerning the joining together of two souls has come our way through all paths of belief, and from many cultures. With each union, more knowledge is gained and more wisdom gathered. Though we are unable to give all this knowledge to these two, who stand before us, we can hope to leave with them the knowledge of love and its strengths and the anticipation of the wisdom that comes with time. The law of life is love unto all beings. Without love, life is nothing, without love, death has no redemption.

Love is anterior to Life, posterior to Death, initial of Creation, and the exponent of Earth. If we learn no more in life, let it be this.

Marriage is a bond to be entered into only after considerable thought and reflection. As with any aspect of life, it has its cycles, its ups and its downs, its trials and its triumphs. With full understanding of this, ____ and ____ have come here today to be joined as one in marriage. Others would ask, at this time, who gives the bride in marriage, but, as a woman is not property to be bought and sold, given and taken, I ask simply if she comes of her own will and if she has her family's blessing.

_____, is it true that you come of your own free will and accord?

BRIDE: Yes, it is true.

Like a stone should your love be firm; like a star should your love be constant. Let the powers of the mind and of the intellect guide you in your marriage, let the strength of your wills bind you together, let the power of love and desire make you happy, and the strength of your dedication make you inseparable. Be close, but not too close. Possess one another, yet be understanding.

Have patience with one another, for storms will come, but they will pass quickly.

Be free in giving affection and warmth. Have no fear and let not the ways of the unenlightened give you unease, for God is with you always.

_____, I have not the right to bind thee to _____, only you have this right. If it be your wish, say so at this time and place your ring in her hand.

GROOM: It is my wish.

OFFICIATE TO BRIDE: _____, if it be your wish for _____ to be bound to you, place the ring on his finger.

Bride places ring on groom's left ring finger.

OFFICIATE: _____, I have not the right to bind thee to _____, only you have

OFFICIATE: With whom do you come and whose blessings accompany you?

FATHER: She comes with me, her father, and is accompanied by all of her family's blessings.

OFFICIATE: Please join hands with your betrothed and listen to that which I am about to say.

Above you are the stars, below you are the stones, as time doth pass, remember …

this right. If it be your wish, say so at this time and place your ring in his hand.

BRIDE: It is my wish.

OFFICIATE TO GROOM: _____, if it be your wish for _____ to be bound to you, place the ring on her finger.

Groom places ring on bride's left ring finger.

OFFICIATE: Repeat after me:

GROOM: I, _____, in the name of the spirit of God that resides within us all, by the life that courses within my blood and the love that resides within my heart, take thee [bride's full name] to my hand, my heart, and my spirit, to be my chosen one. To desire thee and be desired by thee, to possess thee, and be possessed by thee, without sin or shame, for naught can exist in the purity of my love for thee. I promise to love thee wholly and completely without restraint, in sickness and in health, in plenty and in poverty, in life and beyond, where we shall meet, remember, and love again. I shall not seek to change thee in any way. I shall respect thee, thy beliefs, thy people, and thy ways as I respect myself.

BRIDE: I, _____, in the name of the spirit of God that resides within us all, by the life that courses within my blood, and the love that resides within my heart, take thee, [groom's full name] to my hand, my heart, and my spirit to be my chosen one. To desire and be desired by thee, to possess thee, and be possessed by thee, without sin or shame, for naught can exist in the purity of my love for thee. I promise to love thee wholly and completely without restraint, in sickness and in health, in plenty and in poverty, in life and beyond, where we shall meet, remember, and love again. I shall not seek to change thee in any way. I shall respect thee, thy beliefs, thy people, and thy ways as I respect myself.

Officiate hands chalice to the groom:

OFFICIATE: May you drink your fill from the cup of love.

Groom holds chalice to bride while she sips; then bride takes chalice and holds it to groom while he sips. The *chalice is then handed back to the officiate who sets it on the table. Next the officiate takes the plate of bread, giving it to the groom. The same procedure is repeated with bread, groom feeding bride and bride feeding groom.*

By the power vested in me by God and the State, I now pronounce you husband and wife.

May your love so endure that its flame remains a guiding light unto you.

Wiccan Handfasting Ceremony
■ EXAMPLE ■

PRIESTESS SPEAKS: Welcome, friends, as we gather to celebrate the marriage of _____ and _____. Divine One, I ask thee to bless this couple, their love, and their marriage as long as they shall live in love together. May they each enjoy a healthy life filled with joy, love, stability and fertility.

PRIESTESS TURNS TO THE EAST:

Blessed be by the element of air. May you be blessed with communication, intellectual growth, and wisdom.

PRIESTESS TURNS TO THE SOUTH:

Blessed be by the element of fire. May you be blessed with harmony, vitality, creativity, and passion.

PRIESTESS TURNS TO THE WEST:

Blessed be by the element of water. May you be blessed with friendship, intuition, caring, understanding, and love.

PRIESTESS TURNS TO THE NORTH:

Blessed be by the element of earth. May you be blessed with tenderness, happiness, compassion, and sensuality.

PRIESTESS FACES ALL:

In all the eons, the long slow climb of evolution has no greater culmination than the union of people in love. From the time the first amoeba fissioned into two, there has been the possibility of companionship — and the possibility of loneliness.

From the time Nature invented sexual reproduction, love has been a quickening. In humans as self-aware beings, sexuality provided a way that love can conjoin the bodies, hearts, minds, and souls of those who love.

Humans have sadly turned away from Nature's harmony for most of our lives. There is war, loneliness, and desolation, and the soul of Nature mourns. So when there are those of us who love enough to make a commitment such as this one tonight between _____ and _____ the very stars rejoice at the rediscovery of love, joy, and bounty.

Love has its seasons the same as does the Earth. In the spring of love is the discovery of each other, the pulse of the senses, the getting to know the mind and heart of the other; a blooming like the buds and flowers of springtime.

In the summer of love comes the strength, the commitment to each other, the most active part of life, perhaps including the giving of life back to itself through children; the sharing of joys and sorrows, the learning to be humans who are each complete and whole but who can merge each with the other, as the trees grow green and tall in the heat of the sun.

In the fall of love is the contentment of love that knows the other completely. Passion remains, and ease of companionship. The heart smooths love into a steady light, glorious as the autumn leaves.

In the winter of love, there is parting, and sorrow. But love remains, as do the stark and bare tree trunks in the snow, ready for the renewal of love in the spring as life and love begin anew.

Now is the time of summer. _____ and _____ have gathered before their friends to make a statement of their commitment to each other, to their love.

They face each other.

Do you now commit to each other to love, honor, respect each other, to communicate with each other, to look to your own emotional health so that you can relate in a healthy way, and provide a healthy home for children if you choose to have them; to be a support and comfort for your partner in times of sickness and health, as long as love shall last ?

BRIDE & GROOM TOGETHER: We do.

PRIESTESS: Then recite the vows you have written for each other.

The couple moves first to the East, then around the directions.

Couple and Priestess move to a table where sit three candles.

Priestess asks them to each light a candle; they do.

PRIESTESS: These two candles are yourselves. Each of you is a whole and complete human being.

PRIESTESS: _____ speak to us of who you are.

Groom describes himself.

PRIESTESS: _____ speak to us of who you are.

Bride describes herself.

PRIESTESS: Together, light the third candle, but extinguish not the first two. For in marriage you do not lose yourself; you add something new, a relationship, the capacity to merge into one another without losing sight of your individual self.

Together, speak to us of who you are as a couple.

Bride and groom alternate speaking of who they are as a couple.

PRIESTESS: Let us bless the rings.

Circles represent eternity, and though our lives are finite, love is everlasting, the creative force that binds us together, the force that gives new life.

The blessings of the wind upon these rings and your love, that you share communication and creativity.

The blessings of fire upon these rings and your love, that you share passion and the spirit.

The blessings of water upon these rings and your love, that you share love and compassion.

The blessings of the earth upon these rings and your love, that you share health and sexuality.

We humans are born of stardust and deepest oceans, of erupting volcanoes and the bones of the earth.

In celebrating love you celebrate a heritage of all these things, and of the love of all humans from the dawn of time.

In making a commitment to loving each other, you share that which is best in us and give a moment of light to the world.

_____, place the ring on _____ finger and repeat after me:

BRIDE: With this ring, I thee wed.

PRIESTESS: _____, place the ring on _____ hand and repeat after me:

GROOM: With this ring, I thee wed.

PRIESTESS: I now pronounce you married.

May you each and together be blessed with health, happiness, harmony, and love.

So mote it be!

Handfasting & Declaration of Intent
■ EXAMPLE ■

OFFICIATE: Know now before you go further, that since your lives have crossed in this life you have formed ties between each other. As you seek to enter this state of matrimony, you should strive to make real the ideals which give meaning to both this ceremony and the institution of marriage.

With full awareness, know that within this circle you are not only declaring your intent to be handfasted before your friends and family, but you speak that intent also to your creative higher powers.

The promises made today and the ties that are bound here greatly strengthen your union; they will cross the years and lives of each soul's growth. Do you still seek to enter this ceremony?

BRIDE & GROOM TOGETHER: Yes, we seek to enter.

OFFICIATE: In times past it was believed that the human soul shared characteristics with all things divine. It is this belief which assigned virtues to the cardinal directions, East, South, West, and North. It is in this tradition that a blessing is offered in support of this ceremony.

Blessed be this union with the gifts of the East — communication of the heart, mind, and body; fresh beginnings with the rising of each Sun; the knowledge of the growth found in the sharing of silences.

Blessed be this union with the gifts of the South — warmth of hearth and home; the heat of the heart's passion; the light created by both to lighten the darkest of times.

Blessed be this union with the gifts of the West — the deep commitments of the lake; the swift excitement of the river; the refreshing cleansing of the rain; the all–encompassing passion of the sea.

Blessed be this union with the gifts of the North — a firm foundation on which to build; fertility of the fields to enrich your lives; a stable home to which you may always return.

Each of these blessings from the four cardinal directions emphasizes those things which will help you build a happy and successful union. Yet they are only tools — tools which you must use together in order to create what you seek in this union.

I bid you look into each other's eyes.

OFFICIATE: _____, will you cause her pain?

I may.

OFFICIATE: Is that your intent?

GROOM: No.

OFFICIATE: _____, will you cause him pain?

BRIDE: I may.

OFFICIATE: Is that your intent?

BRIDE: No.

OFFICIATE (TO BOTH): Will you share each other's pain and seek to ease it?

BRIDE & GROOM: Yes.

OFFICIATE: And so the binding is made. Join your hands.

First cord is draped across the couple's hands.

OFFICIATE: _____, will you share his laughter?

BRIDE: Yes.

OFFICIATE: _____, will you share her laughter?

GROOM: Yes.

BRIDE: I may.

OFFICIATE: Is that your intent?

BRIDE: No.

OFFICIATE: _____, will you burden her?

GROOM: I may.

OFFICIATE: Is that your intent?

GROOM: No.

OFFICIATE (TO BOTH): Will you share the burdens of each so that your spirits may grow in this union?

BRIDE & GROOM: Yes.

OFFICIATE: And so the binding is made.

Third cord is draped across the couple's hands.

OFFICIATE: _____, will you share his dreams?

BRIDE: Yes.

OFFICIATE: _____, will you share her dreams?

GROOM: Yes.

OFFICIATE (TO BOTH): Will you dream together to create new realities and hopes?

BRIDE & GROOM TOGETHER: Yes.

OFFICIATE: And so the binding is made.

OFFICIATE (TO BOTH): Will both of you look for the brightness in life and the positive in each other?

BRIDE & GROOM: Yes.

OFFICIATE: And so the binding is made.

Second cord is draped across the couple's hands.

OFFICIATE: _____, will you burden him?

Fourth cord is draped across the couple's hands.

OFFICIATE: _____, will you cause her anger?

GROOM: I may.

OFFICIATE: Is that your intent?

GROOM: No.

OFFICIATE: _____, will you cause him anger?

BRIDE: I may.

OFFICIATE: Is that your intent?

BRIDE: No.

OFFICIATE (TO BOTH): Will you take the heat of anger and use it to temper the strength of this union?

BRIDE & GROOM TOGETHER: We will.

OFFICIATE: And so the binding is made.

Fifth cord is draped across the couple's hands.

OFFICIATE: _____, will you honor him?

BRIDE: I will.

OFFICIATE: _____, will you honor her?

GROOM: I will.

OFFICIATE (TO BOTH): Will you seek to never give cause to break that honor?

We shall never do so

OFFICIATE: And so the binding is made.

Sixth cord is draped across the couple's hands.

The officiate ties cords together while saying:

OFFICIATE: The knots of this binding are not formed by these cords but instead by your vows. Either of you may drop the cords, for as always, you hold in your own hands the making or breaking of this union.

Unity Ceremonies

Rose Ceremony

In this ceremony the bride and groom exchange two red roses. This particular rite is at the end of the service in which the bride and groom are pronounced husband and wife.

■ EXAMPLE ■

OFFICIANT: Your gift to each other for your wedding today has been your wedding rings — which shall always be an outward demonstration of your vows of love and respect, and a public showing of your commitment to each other.

You now have what remains the most honorable title that may exist between a man and a woman — the title of "husband" and "wife."

Your first gift to each other as husband and wife will be a single rose.

In the past, the rose was considered a symbol of love, and a single rose always meant only one thing — it meant the words "I love you." So it is appropriate that your first gift as husband and wife is a single rose.

Please exchange your first gift as husband and wife. In some ways it seems like you have not done anything at all. Just a moment ago you were holding one small rose — and now you are holding one small rose. In some ways, a marriage ceremony is like this. In some ways, tomorrow is going to seem no different than yesterday. But in fact today, just now, you both have given and received one of the most valuable and precious gifts of life — one I hope you will always remember — the gift of true and abiding love within the devotion of marriage.

_____ and _____, I would ask that wherever you make your home in the future — whether it be a large and elegant home, or a small and graceful one — that you both pick one very special location for roses; so that on each anniversary of this truly wonderful occasion you may take a rose to that spot both as a recommitment to your marriage, and a recommitment that this will be a marriage based upon love.

In every marriage there are times where it is difficult to find the right words. It is easiest to hurt the one we most love. It is easiest to be most hurt by the one we most love. It might be difficult sometimes to find words to say "I am sorry" or "I forgive you"; "I need you" or "I am hurting." If this should happen, if you simply cannot find these words, leave a rose at that spot that both of you have selected

— for that rose says what matters most of all and should overpower all other things and all other words.

That rose says the words: "I still love you." The other should accept this rose for the words which cannot be found, and remember the love and hope that you both share today.

_____ and _____, if there is anything you remember of this marriage ceremony, it should be that it was love that brought you here today, it is only love that can make it a glorious union, and it is by love that your marriage shall endure.

Unity Candle Ceremony
■ EXAMPLE ■

OFFICIANT: _____ and _____, the two lighted candles symbolize your separate lives, your separate families, and your separate sets of friends. I ask that you each take one candle and, together, light the center candle.

The individual candles represent your individual lives before today. Lighting the center candle represents the joining of your two lives to one light, and the joining together of your two families and sets of friends to one.

Candle Ceremony with Children
■ EXAMPLE ■

OFFICIANT: The lighting of the center candle represents not only the union of _____ and _____ in marriage, but the unity formed in this new family in which your lives will now shine as one family.

And now, let us participate in another symbolic act. Life is full of many such actions that speak to us of a deeper meaning that we cannot always put into words. You have used ancient symbols in this wedding service — the exchange of rings, the clasping of hands, the bearing of flowers.

By such things you act instead of speak in regard to your promises. Now each of you will take a candle. And together you will light one larger candle. This is a vivid reminder that in true Christian marriage our lives are merged, even as we remain individuals. This is a symbolic prayer that God will enhance your own personhood and bless your uniqueness as individuals: but that God will also make of your hands one hand, of your hearts one heart, and of your lives one life.

Unity Sand Ceremony

The Unity sand ceremony is quite similar to the unity candle ceremony in its symbolism. In this ritual, the bride and groom each begin with their own container of sand. As the officiant describes the actions taking place (refer to the language in the unity candle ceremony), the bride and groom simultaneously pour their sand into a single container. The containers should be clear glass so that that visual aspect of two combining into one is clear for all to see. Two different colors of sand can be a nice touch and make for a beautiful and meaningful keepsake for the couple to take home after the ceremony.

The unity sand ceremony might be an especially good option for couples who like the symbolism involved but are not allowed to have lighted candles in their indoor ceremony location, or for those getting married outdoors where the wind may not cooperate in a couple's attempt to keep candles from being blown out.

Same-Sex Unions

Many same-sex couples want the same opportunity as heterosexual partners to affirm their love and make a lasting commitment to each other before friends and family. At the time of this publication, only one state, Massachusetts, permits same-sex marriages; several states sanction civil unions. It may take some searching to find the right person to officiate at a civil union. Unitarian-Universalist ministers will perform civil unions, as will some justices of the peace, nondenominational clergy, and even mayors. A little sleuthing on the Internet will help you locate not only someone to perform the ceremony, but also vendors in your area who will help you plan a celebration as loving and memorable as any wedding.

There is no required wording for a civil union. Many couples, of course, choose to write their own vows, but you can also get ideas from nondenominational vows. You might even want to seal your union by adapting the traditional words that have expressed love and commitment for centuries. Here are a couple of examples:

■ EXAMPLES ■

❧ No. 1

I call upon our families and friends gathered here to witness that I love you. I am committed to our civil union. I promise to be your lover, companion, and friend. Your ally in conflict, your student and teacher. Your comrade in adventure, your consolation in disappointment. Your accomplice in mischief, your strength in your need.

I seek to share with you a relationship of love and humor and tenderness. I will always try to be open and honest with you. I will share my life and my worldly possessions, my thoughts and feelings with you. I will help you fulfill your needs. I will allow you to be yourself. I will rejoice in your growth. I will stand by you through our futures together, respecting you, supporting you, and enjoying you.

❧ No. 2

In the presence of [God and] our family and friends, I, ____, choose you, _____ to be my civil union partner/life partner, to have and to hold from this day forward, for better for worse, for richer for poorer, in sickness and in health, in joy and in sorrow, to love and to cherish, and to be faithful to you alone. This is my solemn vow.

SECOND-TIME MARRIAGE VOWS

■ EXAMPLES ■

❧ No. 1

_____, we take our vows together today. We will be changed forever, and I take them gladly, and without reservation. I promise to honor you, believe in you, protect you, and do everything in my power to make your life happy and fulfilled. This is my promise. Take my hand as we go with joy into our new life together.

❧ No. 2

I am proud to marry you this day, _____. I promise to wipe away your tears with my laughter, and your pain with my caring and my compassion. We will wipe out the old canvases of our lives, and let God, with His amazing artistic talent, fill them with new color, harmony, and beauty. I give myself to you completely, and I promise to love you always, from this day forth.

❧ No. 3

_____, [Life/God] has given us a second chance at happiness. I come today to give you my love, to give you my heart and my hope for our future together. I promise to bring you joy, to be at home with your spirit, and to learn to love you more each day, through all the days of our lives. My love for you is endless and eternal.

❧ No. 4

Because of you, _____, I laugh, I smile, I dare to dream again. I look forward with great joy to spending the rest of my life with you, caring for you, nurturing you, being there for you in all life has for us, and I vow to be true and faithful for as long as we both shall live.

No. 5

Today, as I give myself to you, _____, my mind is clear, and my commitment is strong and without reservation. I take you to be my life's partner. I will never leave you or forsake you; I will spend all my days at your side. We will share a lifetime of eternal, immeasurable love.

No. 6

_____, today I commit myself to years of growth and sharing, as I encourage you to move in a new direction. I will strive to achieve my potential as God's creature, and will celebrate your progress toward the same goal. I give myself to you as I am, and as I will be, and I will do it for all of my life.

No. 7

Respecting each other, _____, we now commit to live our lives together, for all the days to come. I ask you to share this world with me, for good and ill. Be my partner, and I will be yours.

No. 8

_____, may our days be long, and may they be seasoned with love, understanding, and respect.

No. 9

Now we stand together, _____. May it always be so. I offer myself to you today. I will always love you, respect you, and be faithful to you.

No. 10

_____, come health, happiness, and prosperity, I will stand with you, come illness, trouble, or poverty, I will stand with you. Take this ring as a sign of my love and commitment.

No. 11

_____, today I join my life to yours as your friend, your lover, and your confidant. Let me be the shoulder you lean on, the rock on which you rest, the companion of your life. With you I will walk my path from this day forward.

_____, I came here today to join my life to yours before this company. In their presence I pledge to be true to you, to respect you, and to grow with you through the years. Time may pass, fortune may smile, trials may come; no matter what we may encounter together, I vow here that this love will be my only love. I will make my home in your heart from this day forward.

No. 13

Since I have found you, _____, I have found a new life. The decision to commit to share that life with you is one I make happily and with full confidence in our love, secure in the knowledge that you will be my constant friend, my faithful partner in life, and my one true love. On this special day, I give to you, in the presence of [God] and all these witnesses, my pledge to stay by your side, in sickness and in health, in joy and in sorrow, as well as through the good times and the bad. I promise to love you without reservation, comfort you in times of distress, encourage you to achieve all of your goals, laugh with you and cry with you, grow with you in mind and spirit, always be open and honest with you, and cherish you for as long as we both shall live.

Marriage Vows That Blend Families

When children are involved in the blending of a family, it is often important to include them in the wedding ceremony. Following is a sample vow that allows the children to be involved.

BRIDE & GROOM: _____, I promise to be a good and faithful husband/wife to you, and also a patient, loving father/mother to [children's names], caring for them and providing for them as my own. I promise to be their strength and their emotional support, loving them with all my heart forever.

OFFICIANT: And now, [children's names], do you promise to love and respect your parent's new husband/wife? Do you promise to support their marriage and new family? Do you promise to accept the responsibility of being their children, and to encourage them and support them in your new life together?

The children — now part of a blended family — can then respond:

CHILDREN: We do.

RENEWAL OF VOWS

If you decide to renew your wedding vows there are many things to take into consideration. You might want to think about including any children in the vow renewal. It is also customary for the husband to escort the bride down the aisle the second time around. In regard to the bouquet, if at all possible recreate that and the wedding cake and be sure and take another honeymoon, perhaps to the same destination as the first time.

Another fun thing that adds to the ceremony is to display the pictures from the first wedding day celebration.

When thinking about the vows for the renewal ceremony take the time to reflect on your life together thus far, your children or grandchildren ,and where you have been as well as where you are going in the future.

A good time to renew your vows could be on an important anniversary, be it one year, five years or even fifty years, there are no rules.

■ EXAMPLES ■

No. 1

OFFICIANT: When you first joined hands and hearts forty years ago, you did not know where life would take you. You promised to love, honor and cherish one another through all things. Life has surely brought you both wonderful blessings and difficult tribulations. Therefore, you have fulfilled your promise. And God is smiling! So, as you come here today to reaffirm your wedding vows and as you reflect back over all the years as husband and wife, do you now reaffirm the vows you took forty years ago? If so, repeat after me.

A minister may state this declaration of intent, followed by either standard or personal wedding vows.

No. 2

Once before, I stood with you before family and friends; once again, I take your hand as my partner. _____, I take you this day, and for all days, as my husband/wife.

I believe in this marriage more strongly than ever. _____, it is with joy born of experience and trust that I commit myself once again to be your husband/wife.

I, _____, give to you, _____, a new promise, and yet not so new; a new husband/wife, and yet not so new; and a new affirmation of love from the heart that has loved you for _____ years and will love you for as many more as God allots to me.

The couple says "I do" all over again with a wedding vow renewal ceremony.

Quotes a for Vow Renewal

The following is a handful of poignant and appropriate quotes specific to renewal vows. If writing your own renewal vows, you may wish to incorporate one into your words.

Love at first sight is easy to understand; it's when two people have been looking at each other for a lifetime that it becomes a miracle.
Sam Levenson

I love you not only for what you are made of yourself, but for what you are making of me.
Roy Croft

Love is an act of endless forgiveness, a tender look which becomes a habit.
Peter Ustinov

A successful marriage is an edifice that must be rebuilt every day.
André Maurois

Unity, to be real, must stand the severest strain without breaking.
Mahatma Gandhi

Personalized Vows

Writing and reciting your own wedding vows, and perhaps designing part of the ceremony, can be one of the most beautiful things you and your betrothed can do as a couple. There are many ways to go about the process of writing your own vows; the choice depends on you and your personal style.

However, before you begin to deviate from the norm and write your own wedding vows, be sure to discuss this with the official who will be presiding over your wedding ceremony. In many cases, religious requirements prevent couples from creating their own vows. This is more apt to be true if your wedding will be in a church. In addition, many clergy who perform ceremonies do not allow couples to change the wedding vows and will only use the traditional wording for their faith.

Of course, if changing the traditional wedding vows is a problem only for the person performing the ceremony, and not for the location, your alternative is to change officials and find someone who is more open to helping you create the wedding of your dreams.

The main thing to remember is that every denomination has rules and traditions, so find out what those are before planning vows that break them. Moreover, discussing vow limitations with

your clergy might raise faith-based questions that do ultimately need to be discussed.

One important thing to remember is that your vows will not be legally binding unless there is also an "official" vow. This means that you must make a "solemn promise" to stay married to one another.

Writing Your Own Vows

You might start from a romantic standpoint. Sit down with your future spouse and make a list of all those things you want to express to the other person. You already know you love each other and you obviously want to spend the rest of your lives together. You might incorporate any of the following elements into your vows:

favorite songs,

favorite poems,

favorite movie,

favorite book,

things that you and your partner have in common, or

an inside joke.

How do you feel when you laugh together, talk together, or even dance together? What do you love about your partner? These can be romantic or quirky traits, or something in between, but make sure they are genuine and not clichés. Everyone knows you think she is the sweetest person in the world, or you wouldn't be marrying her. Likewise, most people will already believe you think he is a good provider or you would not have said "yes" to his proposal. Answer the following questions about your partner:

When did you know this person was "the one?"

What do you find irresistible or unique about your partner?

What does your partner hate or love about himself/herself?

What are your dreams together?

What was your engagement like?

How have you changed since you met your partner?

How have your dreams been fulfilled with your partner?

How have each of you enriched each other's lives?

How will your life change being married to this person?

You might also consider writing your wedding vows based on a timeline, highlighting the past, present, and future in special ways. Here are some tips. Ask yourself:

What were you looking for in a mate when you met your partner?

Describe the first time you met.

Describe that first kiss — where were you?

What has been the most difficult part of your relationship?

What are your dreams for the future?

What are your promises to one another?

You'll need to decide whether you and your partner will use the same vows or individualize them. If you are each writing your own words of love, think about common themes and discuss the length of the vows. From there you can write your vows separately and come together with them on your wedding day. Following are examples you can use as inspiration:

■ EXAMPLES ■

❧No. 1

Love has given us wings, and our journey begins today.

_____, wherever the wind may carry me,

I will stay by your side as your husband/wife,

Take this ring as a sign of my love.

❧No. 2

Where there has been cold, you have brought warmth; where my life was dark, you have brought light.

❧No. 3

_____, I pledge before this assembled company to be your husband/wife from this day forward. Let us make of our two lives, one life, and let us always honor and respect each other.

No. 4

_____, our miracle lies in the path we have chosen together.

I enter this marriage with you knowing that the true magic of love is not to avoid changes, but to navigate them successfully. Let us commit to the miracle of making each day work — together.

No. 5

Whatever lies ahead, good or bad, we will face together. Distance may test us for a time, and time may try us. But if we look to each other first, we will always see a friend.

_____, look to me for all the days to come; today I take my place as your husband/wife.

No. 6

On this day, [month, day, year], I, _____, join myself to you, _____, before this company.

May our days be long, and may they be seasoned with love, understanding, and respect.

The following is an example of personalized wedding vows in which the bride and groom express their feelings in a back and forth manner:

BRIDE: When I was a young I always believed that I would get married, have children, and live happily ever after. I believed that I would be swept away by a man who knew everything about me and who could read my mind. As I grew older, I realized that I too was responsible for making that dream a reality, but it was hard to do that until finally I met you.

GROOM: I promise to always do my best to give you all of the love and appreciation that you have given to me and to always hold you dear for all that you are.

Your vows can go back and forth until you have expressed all those things that the two of you want to share with one another.

Incorporating poems or songs (partial or complete) into your personalized vows may help you to express your personal feelings clearly. The best way to transition to the poetry is to have the official begin the ceremony and announce what you and your partner will be reading. Elizabeth Barrett Browning is often quoted in wedding ceremonies, and verse XIV from _Sonnets from the Portuguese_ is a wonderful choice:

If thou must love me, let it be for nought

Except for love's sake only. Do not say

"I love her for her smile — her look — her way
Of speaking gently, — for a trick of thought

That falls in well with mine, and certes brought

A sense of pleasant ease on such a day" —

For these things in themselves, Beloved, may

Be changed, or change for thee, — and love, so wrought,

May be unwrought so. Neither love me for

Thine own dear pity's wiping my cheeks dry, —

A creature might forget to weep, who bore

Thy comfort long, and lose thy love thereby!

But love me for love's sake, that evermore

Thou mayst love on, through love's eternity.

Another option is this selection from the *I Ching*:

When two people are at one

in their inmost hearts,

They shatter even the strength of iron or of bronze.

And when two people understand each other in their inmost hearts,

Their words are sweet and strong

like the fragrance of orchids.

No poem selection would be complete without these lines from Robert Burns's "A Red, Red Rose":

O my luve is like a red, red rose,

That's newly sprung in June:

O my luve is like the melodie,

That's sweetly played in tune.

As fair art thou, my bonnie lass,

So deep in luve am I;

And I will luve thee still, my dear,

Till a' the seas gang dry.

Till a' the seas gang dry, my dear,

And the rocks melt wi' the sun;

And I will luve thee still my dear,

While the sands o' life shall run.

And fare thee weel, my only luve!

And fare thee weel a while!

And I will come again, my luve,

Tho' it were ten thousand mile.

Other poems that might be meaningful are Shakespeare's "Sonnet 18," Lord Byron's "She Walks in Beauty," Elizabeth Barrett Browning's "How Do I Love Thee," or William Penn's "Never Marry but for Love."

The Bible is also full of beautiful lines and verses that can help express joy and love in Christian wedding vows. Here are a few you may want to include in your ceremony.

Place me like a seal over your heart, like a seal on your arm; for love is as strong as death, its jealousy unyielding as the grave. It burns like a blazing fire, like a mighty flame. Many waters cannot quench love; rivers cannot wash it away. If one were to give all the wealth of his house for love, it would be utterly scorned.

Song of Solomon 8

Two are better than one, because they have a good return for their toil. For if they fall, one will lift up his fellow; but woe to him who is alone when he falls and has not another to lift him up.

Again, if two lie together, they are warm; but how can one be warm alone? And though a man might prevail against one who is alone, two will withstand him.

Ecclesiastes 4:9–12

Other scriptures to consider are I Corinthians 13, John 15:12–14, I John 4:18, Colossians 3:12–14, and Proverbs 18:22. An option from the Koran is 30:21.

Reciting Your Own Vows in the Ceremony

Once you have chosen the words you will recite, the next step is practicing them. Often reciting the vows in front of the audience at your wedding will be harder than writing them, but practice will ease your anxiety.

The first thing to decide is whether you will memorize your vows or read them from a piece of paper. If you decide to memorize the vows, you must do it naturally or not at all. If you already know you are not good at memorization, reading them is fine; just present your vows in a way that you know you will be comfortable with.

PART TWO

WEDDING TOASTS

Speaking in public is never easy, and certainly not in front of a room of people who are more than likely expecting something lighthearted and witty. Whether you are the best man, the bride's father, the maid of honor, or the groom himself, making that celebratory toast is a sure way to get the palms sweating like nothing else you have ever experienced.

To make it easier, start with the simple fact that everyone wants you to do well. The good feelings and well wishes that generally go with a wedding mean you are already playing to a receptive audience. So as long as you don't say anything embarrassing in your toast, chances are your special words will go over without a hitch.

Of course, it's always a good idea to have an idea of what you plan to say. Never just stand up in a crowded room and start rambling without any clear direction. This is a recipe for disaster, so start out with a "cheat sheet" and make your short time in front of the microphone work for you.

It seems easy enough — you begin by raising your glass, you look around the room, and then you deliver the best speech you have ever given in your life. However, start preparing for your toast early so you don't end up being too long-winded, wordy, or trite.

The number one rule when making a toast is not to be boring! The toast should be short and sweet — anywhere from thirty seconds to one minute — with words of wisdom, a possible rhyme or quotation, and a personal touch that will assure people remember your toast long after you sit down.

Truly heartfelt wedding toasts should convey special feelings for the occasion while also expressing the feelings of everyone in the room. Humor also makes a toast memorable, and even though a toast might be short, it can spark a laugh as well as tug at the heartstrings. The final impor-

tant thing to remember to deliver a great toast (besides keeping it brief, but never boring) is to make sure you speak loud enough for everyone in the room to hear you. Get a good laugh, incorporate a sentimental element, offer up the proper thank-you, and do it with all of the graciousness you can offer.

Before the big day, practice your toast alone in front of a mirror so that as you stand in front of the crowded room, you know exactly what to say, when to raise your glass, and when to end your toast with that sparkling bit of panache that would make a toastmaster proud.

Toasting Etiquette

The idea of offering a toast is believed to have originated many years ago, when poisoning a person by slipping something into his glass was quite popular. To alleviate this problem, hosts began to pour drinks from a pitcher from which everyone drank, thereby demonstrating that the liquid being offered was not poison. Eventually, this tradition became a part of wedding festivities, and the rest is history.

The first tenet of toasting in any situation is to keep it short. The wedding is not about the toaster, but the couple being toasted. That means you really don't have to do much more than offer your congratulations, perhaps tell a brief story, and hand the mike to the next person.

Usually the master of ceremonies for the toasts is the best man. People often believe the band leader or disc jockey assumes this role, but this is not true. Because they may have to stick to a schedule, the couple will want to determine early on who will be offering toasts at the wedding reception. This varies depending on the situation, and there are no hard and fast rules. Of course, the best man needs to toast the bride, the maid/matron of honor should toast the groom, and the father of the bride will almost always toast the couple. It is also standard fare for the bride and groom to toast their parents and the guests. After those toasts, the rest is just a matter of preference.

Toasts are also appropriate at the rehearsal dinner. This is a great time for all those extra toasts that there might not be time for at the wedding reception. When a toast is given at a formal affair, it is normally done after the meal. At the reception, if the wedding cake is being served as the dessert, then the toast comes after the cutting of the cake. When the cake is not the dessert, toasts usually occur right after the meal. In the case of a less formal wedding reception, the toast is made after the couple's first dance together.

When you know you will be asked to give a toast at a wedding reception or wedding-related function, remember these guidelines:

🌿 Don't go unprepared. Plan ahead and know what you will say.

🌿 Speak from the heart. Don't try to be someone you are not; this is your personal tribute. Saying what is in your heart will mean more to the couple.

🌿 Be brief.

🌿 Don't embarrass the couple you are toasting.

🌿 Practice what you will say, and remember — you will likely be holding the glass in one hand and a microphone in the other.

🌿 Don't drink too much before you give your toast.

🌿 Look at the couple as you deliver the toast and be sincere in your expression.

At the end of the toast, everyone in attendance will take a drink. A sip is all that is necessary. If a guest absolutely cannot drink alcohol, another beverage should be supplied, as it is considered bad luck if all the guests do not join in the toast.

Preparing and Delivering the Toast

Preparing just the right toast is very important and should not be taken lightly. Toasts are a part of the wedding celebration that will be remembered for years to come.

Before you sit down to write your toast, think about what you want to say — what are the highlights? Once you have a draft, change any words or phrases that you repeat too many times — you're aiming for a toast that is genuine but also clever, catchy, and unique. What's more, be sure you know the proper pronunciation of any names you might be mentioning. Keep in mind the other tips listed on page 110 and you'll be well prepared.

Before you get started, take a few deep breaths. Look toward the couple you are toasting and speak to them as if they are the only other people in the room. Talk slowly and clearly so everyone can hear. Most likely everyone will have stopped talking to give you their attention, and you will probably have a microphone in one hand. Just make sure you don't cause any feedback to deafen the crowd. Also, check that the microphone is on before you begin your toast!

If you get nervous, don't drink to soothe your nerves before your toast. Unfortunately, that may only make things worse. There is a good chance that no one will notice how nervous you are; after all, the wedding is not about the guests, but about the couple getting married.

All toasts should have a beginning, middle, and end. Following are some basic highlights for each part; the example is for the best man.

Beginning

At the beginning of the toast you should introduce yourself. This will immediately break the ice and help propel you into your speech. If some people in the crowd are still talking, very politely tap on your glass and say, "excuse me." Then give everyone a chance to finish their conversations before you begin.

Remember to thank the people hosting the event, usually the parents of the bride. If the bride and groom are hosting themselves, you might just say, "We're all delighted to be here today on this joyous occasion."

Here's an example:

I would now like to propose a toast to the happy couple. They seem more in love with each passing day.

Let me start by thanking Mr. and Mrs._____ for allowing us all to share in this very important occasion in their lives, the marriage of their daughter, _____. Let me also thank (the groom) for his generosity of spirit in finally acknowledging that I am the best man.

Middle

Next comes the middle part to your toast. This can be a funny story or anecdote about the bride and groom. You might say a few things on love and marriage or even about how the two met. Were you there when they met? Did you always know she was the one for your best friend? Be sincere and heartfelt and you will inevitably say the right thing.

Closing

End the toast with a wish or a blessing for the couple. Here are two examples:

❧ No. 1

Let us congratulate _____ and _____ for taking this significant step, and let us wish them all happiness from this day forward. Ladies and gentlemen, please rise and join me in drinking a toast to the bride and groom.

❧ No. 2

Let me tell you, _____, you couldn't be luckier. _____ is such a beautiful, gracious and kind woman and I wish you both well, and may all your troubles be little ones. So I raise my glass to honor you with a smile in my heart, and I ask you all, ladies and gentlemen, to do likewise. Please rise and drink a toast to the lovely bride and her lucky groom!

USING PROPS FOR YOUR TOAST

Sometimes having a prop as you offer a toast is a good idea. In many cases this simply means having notes. Notes offer a comfort level that you might well need when standing in front of the audience. You can use notes in many different ways, from jotting down a few key words to writing the entire toast. However, be sure you put the notes in a place that will be easy to find, such as your jacket pocket. If you are right-handed, place your notes in your right-hand outside pocket, and visa versa if you are left-handed. For women this is easier — just put the notes in your purse until your times comes to make the toast.

Be sure you can read your writing — often the lights are dim and you might be nervous, so take precautions early. Likewise, don't use paper that will rattle when you take it from your pocket or hold it while reading; this will be very distracting for both you and the audience. Index cards can be a good idea, but don't get them in the wrong order or you may deliver a very confusing toast.

Another good ready-made prop is the microphone or a glass of champagne or wine. You will need to raise this at the end of your toast anyway, when you ask everyone to take a drink with you.

# When to Toast

A wedding toast might be offered at several events other than the wedding reception: the engagement party, bridal or couple's shower, bachelor or bachelorette party, the rehearsal dinner, and perhaps a wedding breakfast.

ENGAGEMENT PARTY

The engagement party is usually held as a way to introduce the couple's families to one another and, in some cases, to display the bride's ring. The father of the bride-to-be usually makes the formal announcement of the engagement. It is also common for the host — usually the father of the bride — to have the guest's glasses filled so that he can propose a toast to the couple.

After the parents toast the couple, either the bride or groom should make a toast in return. Often the groom will offer a brief toast after the father of the bride. Then it is time for the bride-to-be to toast her fiancé. It is here that a favorite quote or poem is quite appropriate to begin the toast.

BRIDAL OR COUPLE'S SHOWER

A toast for the bride at the bridal shower is a wonderful way to get everything going. At the bridal or couple's shower there are many ways to celebrate the couple or the bride alone. Remember, the shower it is not about the gifts received or the games played, but about the touching words and unique acts of love and appreciation by family and friends.

BACHELOR AND BACHELORETTE PARTIES

Toasts are often given at bachelor parties. In the past, when bachelor parties were traditionally more formal affairs, the groom would stand as the dinner was ending and offer a toast "to the bride." The groom's friends would then stand and do the same thing, and everyone would break their glasses. Nowadays, bachelor party speeches may begin something like this: "We are here to say goodbye to our friend _____, who is departing for the land of the married."

Rehearsal Dinner

Rehearsal dinners are very common occasions for toasts. The dinner is almost always hosted by the groom's parents and takes place the night before the wedding. The people invited to the rehearsal dinner are those in the wedding and their spouses or significant others, plus a few very close friends. As a rule, out-of-town guests do not need to be invited, but this depends on the couple and how far the guests have come to attend the celebration.

Traditionally, toasts at the rehearsal dinner begin when the first course is served. The host will welcome the guests and thank the bride's parents for hosting the wedding. The father of the bride then responds with his own toasts, as do the groom, the groomsmen, and perhaps a few of the bridesmaids. Of course, there is nothing wrong with anyone else at the dinner offering a toast from the bride's mother to an out-of-town guest.

WEDDING RECEPTION

The wedding reception is where the best man has a chance to shine. He is in charge of the first toast and will need to get everyone's attention as the toasts and speeches begin. The following sequence is the normal order that toasts are given at the wedding reception:

1. Best man
2. Groom's father
3. Bride's father
4. Groom
5. Bride
6. Friends and relatives
7. Maid/matron of honor
8. Groom's mother
9. Bride's mother
10. Anyone else

WEDDING BREAKFAST

The wedding breakfast is usually held after the marriage ceremony and is a wonderful way for all the family and friends to say goodbye. It is here that perhaps final toasts can be offered as the couple begin their new life together.

Sample Toasts

Members of the wedding party and often guests are called upon or volunteer to address a toast to the couple. More often than not, this occurs at the wedding reception, but, as mentioned earlier, there are always other opportunities for celebrating the bride and groom. Following are a few openers that may inspire you to create your own.

Toasts to the Bride

• Here's to the bride — may she share everything with her husband . . . and that includes the housework!

• May we never forget what is worth remembering or remember what is best forgotten.

Toasts to the Bride or Groom by the Spouse

• Here's to the prettiest/handsomest, here's to the wittiest, here's to the truest of all who are true,
Here's to the neatest one, here's to the sweetest one,
Here's to them, all in one — here's to you.

• Here's to my bride/groom: she/he knows everything about me, yet loves me just the same.

• Merry met, and merry part, I drink to thee with all my heart.

• (Groom), take (Bride)'s hand and place your hand over hers. Now, remember this moment and cherish it . . . because this will be the last time you'll ever have the upper hand!

• I have known many, liked not a few, Loved only one: I toast to you.

Toasts to the Groom

• Here's to the groom, a man who keeps his head though he loses his heart.

• May your voyage through life be as happy and as free as the dancing waves on the deep blue sea.

• May your love be added, may it never be subtracted, may your household multiply, and may your hearts never be divided!

Toasts to the Couple

- May the most you wish for be the least you get.

- Here's to the new husband, and here's to the new wife, may they remain lovers, for all of life.

- May you both live as long as you want, And never want as long as you live.

- Happy marriages begin when we marry the one we love, and they blossom when we love the one we married.

- May your troubles be less And your blessings be more. And nothing but happiness Come through your door.

- My greatest wish for the two of you is that through the years your love for each other will so deepen and grow, that years from now you will look back on this day, your wedding day, as the day you loved each other the least.

- May the roof above you never fall in, and may you both never fall out.

- May we all be invited to your golden wedding celebration?

- Coming together is a beginning; keeping together is progress; working together is success.

- When you are wrong, admit it and when you are right, keep quiet!

- May you have many children and may they grow mature in taste and healthy in color and as sought after as the contents of the glass.

- Remember that if you ever put your marital problems on the back burner they are sure to boil over.

- To the lamp of love — may it burn brightest in the darkest hours and never flicker in the winds of trial.

- May "for better or worse" be better than worse.

- The man or woman you really love will never grow old to you. Through the wrinkles of time, through the bowed frame of years, you will always see the dear face and feel the warm heart union of your eternal love.

- May you be poor in misfortune,
Rich in blessings,
Slow to make enemies,
And quick to make friends.
But rich or poor,
Quick or slow,
May you know nothing but happiness

From this day forward.

- Here's to health and prosperity,
To you and all your posterity.
And them that doesn't drink with sincerity,
That they may be damned for all eternity!

- May the joys you share today be the beginning of a lifetime of great happiness and fulfillment.

- May the love you've expressed to each other today always be the first thoughts during any trying times in the future.

Toasts by the Parents

- It is written: when children find true love, parents find true joy. Here's to your joy and ours, from this day forward. We toast to you!

Toasts by the Best Man

See *Toasts to the Couple* for numerous ideas. The following is a longer speech from the best man to a bride and groom getting married for the second time; it may provide some inspiration. Other examples follow.

- Good evening. My name is _____, and on behalf of _____ and _____, I want to thank everyone for celebrating this joyous occasion with them. I am thrilled that I am with these two wonderful people as they begin this new chapter in their lives.

This is an especially eventful day because it offers _____ and _____ each a second chance at happiness. What a wonderful day of hope and joy, peace and contentment. These two have walked many miles to be here together today, and this wedding is a joy to behold. I can speak for everyone in this room when I say we all wish you the happiness that you deserve. We are so glad that you have found one another, and this day is a reminder that the best is yet to come. Your marriage to each other is a true triumph of hope over experience. It's been said that if marriage is to be a success, one should begin by marrying the right person.

I don't think I've ever seen a couple who complement each other as much as these two do. [Personal anecdote about the bride and groom here]

They say that there is no surprise as magical as finding your life's mate later in life. You two must feel the magic, because it seems as if your happiness emanates from you on this very magical day!

• A good marriage is at least 80 percent good luck in finding the right person at the right time. The rest is trust.

• A successful marriage requires falling in love many times, always with the same person. Seek a happy marriage with wholeness of heart, but do not expect to reach the Promised Land without going through some wilderness together.

Toasts by the Maid of Honor

If the maid of honor speaks, she will speak after the best man and basically offers a short toast. She will say how she met the bride, how they became friends, and perhaps offer a funny story. She also wishes the couple a wonderful life together.

Toasts by the Bride

• On behalf of _____ and myself, I would like to thank you all for joining us today as we celebrate our marriage. I know that some of you have traveled many miles to be here — thank you. We are honored to have you with us. As I look around me, I am reminded of the importance of family and friends. _____ and I are truly blessed in having all of you with us today to share in this joyous occasion — to witness our union and the coming together of our two families. Thank you all for your support and your love.

Toasts by the Groom

The groom usually offers toasts on behalf of himself and his new bride. He thanks the bride's parents and relative as well as his own family He also thanks the best man and groomsmen. Finally, he thanks all the guests for attending the wedding celebration.

To the bride: Family, friends, members of the wedding party, I give you — my beautiful bride.

I knew from the moment I saw _____ that she was my soul mate. _____, you're beautiful inside and out.

To the parents of the bride: To _____ and _____, I thank you for including me in your family and for thinking of me as one of your own.

To THE PARENTS OF THE GROOM: How can I ever thank you for all your love and support? You have always been there for me and I celebrate you with a toast.

To THE WEDDING GUESTS: Let the celebration begin! I am honored that each of you are here to be part of this special day.

To THE BEST MAN: It's great to see the best man dressed for something other than a court appearance!

To THE GROOMSMEN: I have shared many memories with each and everyone of you and I thank you for being part of this incredible day with _____ (bride's name) and me. It means a lot to us for you to be here.

How to Use Jokes, Anecdotes, and Quotes

Sometimes a good joke or anecdote is the perfect solution to your dilemma of what to say as you raise your glass for a toast. If you aren't the best joke teller, stick to one-liners. There is nothing worse than telling a joke that ends with dead silence in the room. Try your joke out on someone before the wedding — you will thank yourself.

There are many places to find good jokes. Start with a book; think about jokes a favorite comedian has told in the past; ask your funny friends for advice on what to say. Finally, don't hesitate to turn to a professional speech writer if you need more help. When you are putting together a funny story remember that the humor lies in the punch line which usually contains an element of surprise. You can also go from uplifting to ridiculous or from exhilaration to despair. These are the elements that will make your joke worth telling.

If you decide to include anecdotes, make them short and be sure they are amusing enough to tell. You can also consider a witty quotation or poem, but remember that you also need an opening and a closing.

FUNNY WEDDING TOASTS

• To the two secrets of a long-lasting and happy marriage — Here's to a good sense of humor and a short memory!

• Never go to bed angry . . . always stay up and argue.

• Always remember the three little words . . . "You're right dear."

• Early in your marriage you will find it difficult to get the last word in any discussion. With time, though, you will learn how to always get the last two words in every discussion — just make sure the words are "Yes, dear."

• Marriage is like a violin. After the music is over, you still have the strings.

QUOTES TO USE IN TOASTS

Quotes are always useful when making a toast. In fact, you can never go wrong by using just the right quote at the right time while you are proposing your toast to the couple.

Popular Quotes

• Marriage is not a ritual or an end. It is a long, intricate, intimate dance together and nothing matters more than your own sense of balance and your choice of partner.

Amy Bloom

• The only gift is a portion of thyself.

Ralph Waldo Emerson

• That life is only life forevermore, together wing to wing and oar to oar.

Robert Frost

• Love is what makes two people sit in the middle of a bench when there is plenty of room at both ends.

Anonymous

• Marriage, ultimately, is the practice of becoming passionate friends.

Harville Hendrix

• There is nothing more admirable than two people who see eye-to-eye keeping house as man and wife, confounding their enemies, and delighting their friends.

Homer (updated version)

• The most powerful symptom of love is a tenderness which becomes at times almost insupportable.

Victor Hugo

• Here's to marriage, that happy estate that resembles a pair of scissors: So joined that they cannot be separated, often moving in opposite directions, yet punishing anyone who comes between them.

Sydney Smith

• Marriage is popular because it combines the maximum of temptation with the maximum of opportunity.

George Bernard Shaw

• Happiness in marriage is entirely a matter of chance.

Jane Austen

• Whatever you do . . . love those who love you.

Voltaire

• Love and marriage, go together like a horse and carriage.

Sammy Cahn, song

• Whoever loved that loved not at first sight?

Christopher Marlowe

• And to his eye, there was but one beloved face on earth, and that was shining on him.

Lord Byron

• A thing of beauty is a joy forever.

John Keats

• The meeting of two personalities is like the contact of two chemical substances; if there is any reaction, both are transformed.

Carl Jung

• Love does not consist in gazing at each other, but in looking outward in the same direction.

Antoine de Saint-Exupéry

• The secret of a happy marriage remains a secret.

Henny Youngman

• Nobody will ever win the battle of the sexes. There's too much fraternizing with the enemy.

Anonymous

• To love is to receive a glimpse of heaven.

Karen Sunde

• A good marriage is like a casserole; only those responsible for it really know what goes in it.

Anonymous

• Sweet is the dream, divinely sweet, when absent souls in fancy meet.

Sir Thomas More

• You know when you have found your prince because you not only have a smile on your face, but in your heart as well.

Anonymous

• There is no remedy for love but to love more.

Henry David Thoreau

• For it was not into my ear you whispered, but into my heart. It was not my lips that you kissed but my soul.

Judy Garland

• For those passionately in love, the whole world seems to smile.

David Myers

• Some people say there are plenty of fish in the sea, until you find love — then there is only one.

David Baird

• A heart that loves is always young.

Greek proverb

• Couples who love each other tell each other a thousand things without talking.

Chinese Proverb

• My greatest good fortune in a life of brilliant experience has been to find you.

Winston Churchill

Funny Quotes

• Some people fall in love by slipping on the same banana skin.

Lisa Swerling and Ralph Lazar

• One is very crazy when in love.

Sigmund Freud

• I love being married. It's so great to find that one special person you want to annoy for the rest of your life.

Rita Rudner

• Always get married early in the morning. That way, if it doesn't work out, you haven't wasted a whole day.

Mickey Rooney

• Marriage is when a man and woman become as one; the trouble starts when they try to decide which one.

Anonymous

• Adam and Eve had an ideal marriage. He didn't have to hear about all the men she could have married... and she didn't have to hear about how well his Mother cooked.

Anonymous

• Love is like an hourglass, with the heart filling up as the brain empties.

Jules Renard

Quotes for Second Marriages

• I chose my wife, as she did her wedding gown, for qualities that would wear well.

Oliver Goldsmith

• The triumph of hope over experience.

Dr. Samuel Johnson

• And on her lover's arm she leant,
And round her waist she felt it fold,
And far across the hills they went
In that new world which is the old.

Alfred Lord Tennyson

• . . . speak of one that loved not wisely but too well; of one not easily jealous, but being wrong perplex'd in the extreme.

William Shakespeare

Index